MW00427330

You Will Be
Changed into Me

You Will Be Changed into Me

The Fruits of the Eucharist

Stuart Squires

NEW CITY PRESS
Enkindling the Spirit of Unity

Published by New City Press
202 Comforter Blvd.,Hyde Park, NY 12538
www.newcitypress.com
©2024 Stuart Squires

You Will Be Changed into Me
The Fruits of the Eucharist
Stuart Squires

Springsteen
Words and Music by Eric Church, Jeffery Hyde and Ryan Tyndell
Copyright ©2011 Sony Music Publishing (US) LLC, Sinnerlina
Music, BMG Bumblebee, Mammaw's Combread Music and Anthem
Music Publishing I
All Rights on behalf of Sony Music Publishing (US) LLC and
Sinnerlina Music Administered by Sony Music Publishing (US) LLC,
424 Church Street, Suite 1200, Nashville, TN 37219
All Rights on behalf of BMG Bumblebee and Mammaw's Combread
Music Administered by BMG Rights Management (US) LLC
International Copyright Secured All Rights Reserved
Reprinted by Permission of Hal Leonard LLC

Layout and design by Miguel Tejerina
Cover design by Maria Oswalt

Library of Congress Control Number: 2023947777

ISBN: 978-1-56548-586-0 (paper)
ISBN: 978-1-56548-587-7 (e-book)

Printed in the United States of America

For Andy,
whose hand was on my shoulder
the first time I received the Eucharist

Contents

Introduction

In recent decades, countless Catholic books have been written that focus on the question of the nature of the Eucharist. What, they ask, is it? Is Jesus physically present in the Eucharist? Is he sacramentally present? Is he spiritually present? Is he really present? Is the Eucharist merely a symbol? Interest in the question of Jesus' presence in the Eucharist persists because of the continuing debate between Catholics and Protestants that has been simmering since the Reformation. For five hundred years, Catholics and Protestants have disagreed (sometimes violently) over the answer to this question. In light of Protestant assertions that the communion wafer (as many Protestants call it) is a symbol of Jesus or represents Jesus (among other nuanced answers), these Catholic books emphasize that the Catholic Church teaches that Christ's body, blood, soul, and divinity are "truly, really, and substantially" present in the Eucharist.

Although this question of the nature of the Eucharist is historically and theologically important, it unfortunately has overshadowed a question that is just as important, if not more important: what does the Eucharist *do*? If the Eucharist were nothing more than a symbol, all it would do is point to something outside itself. If, as Catholics believe, Jesus is really present in the Eucharist, then we should expect that the Eucharist does something. It does, in fact, many things.

This book will introduce six of the most important fruits, or effects, of the Eucharist. It will explore how the Jesus Event is brought to the present through eucharistic memory; it will investigate how the Eucharist is the application of Christ's sacrificial offering on the cross; it will demonstrate how the Eucharist transforms the communicant; it will review how the unity in the human family is created by the Eucharist through union with Christ; it will show how the Eucharist leads to a life that seeks justice; it will explain the significance of the Eucharist for the journey beyond this life.

The answers to our main question—what does the Eucharist do?—are relevant to every Catholic in the pews. They directly address the pressing question many young Catholics (and even adult Catholics) are asking today: why should I go to Mass when I find it uninspiring? The answers that young Catholics often receive are some variations of "because I said so," or "because we are Catholic, and that is what we do," or "because your grandmother would be upset if we don't go." Although these answers may be true, they are banal, and, in the long run, unlikely to foster in anyone a commitment to receive and cooperate with Jesus' transformative grace in the Eucharist. I hope that an appreciation of the fruits of the Eucharist described in this book will lead to a deeper desire to encounter Christ in the host and chalice.

Chapter One

The Real Presence of Jesus in the Eucharist

My flesh is true food, and my blood is true drink.

Jesus, in the Bread of Life Discourse

Introduction

An oft-cited vignette that summarizes the Catholic under-standing of the nature of the Eucharist comes from a letter by one of the most important Catholic fiction writers of the twentieth century—Flannery O'Connor.[1] Around 1950, the poet Robert Lowell and the novelist Elizbeth Hardwick took O'Connor to a dinner party with the author Mary McCarthy and her husband. Five hours into the party, the shy O'Connor had yet to say a word, as she did not feel that she had anything to contribute to the conversation. She felt as if she were a dog "who had been trained to say a few words but overcome with inadequacy had forgotten them." Eventually, the conversa-tion turned towards the Eucharist, and McCarthy, who had abandoned Catholicism as a teenager, said that when she was a child, she had thought of the Eucharist as the Holy Spirit because it was the "most portable" of the three persons of the Trinity. Now, as an adult, McCarthy thought of the Eucharist as a pretty good symbol. Her voice trembling, O'Connor shot back: "Well, if it's a symbol, to hell with it."[2]

Usually with less spicy language, the Catholic Church has echoed O'Connor's sentiment through time. The Eucharist is more than a symbol. It is "truly, really, and substantially"[3] the body, blood, soul, and divinity of Jesus Christ—a theological mouthful usually shortened to the phrase the "real presence" of Jesus in the Eucharist. Most Catholics today, however, seem to have no idea that this is what the Catholic Church has taught for two thousand years. A 2019 Pew Research Center study found that 69 percent of self-identified Catholics believe that, after the consecration, the bread and the wine "are symbols of the body and blood of Jesus Christ."[4] Only 31 percent acknowledge that the bread and wine "actually become the body and blood of Jesus."[5] In light of the Church's emphasis of the real presence of Christ in the Eucharist, and the ease of finding the authentic Catholic teaching in books or on the internet, it is shocking that so many Catholics do not know what the Church actually teaches. Or, as Bishop Robert Barron put it sharply, this study is "deeply disturbing," and demonstrates a "massive failure on the part of the Church carrying on its own Tradition."[6]

This chapter will survey some of the most important biblical, theological, and conciliar attestations to Jesus' real presence in the Eucharist. It will begin by exploring three passages from the Old Testament concerning God's presence to his people: in the Tabernacle, in the Temple, and in the Bread of the Presence. It then will survey how God's presence in the Tabernacle, in the Temple, and in the Bread of the Presence continues in Jesus himself. Finally, it will review some important examples from the Tradition that reiterate the Church's teaching of the real presence. As this book is primarily interested in investigating the fruits of the Eucharist, this will be the shortest chapter because many other books explore the real presence in detail.[7]

Old Testament

Although the Old Testament offers many examples of God's "overshadowing presence" to his people (in Hebrew *shekinah*, from the verb *shachan* meaning "to dwell or abide"),[8] we will focus on three: God's presence in the Tabernacle, in the Temple, and in the Bread of the Presence.

When the Israelites had been liberated from slavery in Egypt, God told Moses to have the Israelites "make a sanctuary for me, that I may dwell in their midst" (Ex 25:8). During their years of wandering in the desert, this sanctuary, otherwise known as the Tent of Meeting, or Tabernacle (in Latin *tabernaculum*, which means "tent"), housed the Ark of the Covenant, which contained the tablets of the Ten Commandments, a jar of manna, and the rod of Aaron. God then described how the Ark should be constructed. Among other details, he commanded that the "mercy seat" be placed atop the Ark. God would "meet you [Moses] there," and would "tell you all that I command you regarding the Israelites" (Ex 25:21-22).

God later commanded the Israelites to offer a sacrifice at the entrance of the Tabernacle where God "will meet you and speak to you" (Ex 29:42). There, the altar would be made sacred by God's glory. "Thus," God said, "I will consecrate the Tent of Meeting and the altar. . . I will dwell in the midst of the Israelites and will be their God. They shall know that I, the Lord, am their God who brought them out of the land of Egypt, so that I, the Lord, their God might dwell among them" (Ex 29:43-46). After God's orders had been completed, the "column of cloud" (Ex 33:9-10) covered the Tabernacle, and "the glory of the Lord filled the Tabernacle." Moses could not enter because the cloud settled down upon it and the glory of the Lord filled it. Whenever the cloud lifted, the Israelites would resume their journey. "Only when it lifted did they move forward. The cloud of the Lord was over the Tabernacle by day, and fire in the cloud at night, in the sight of the whole house of Israel in all the stages of their journey [through the desert]" (Ex 40:37-38).

After the monarchy had been established under King Saul, David, the second king, intended to construct the Temple, the permanent place on earth where God resides. But the Lord would not allow him to build it because he had shed much blood and waged many wars. David's son, Solomon, constructed the first Temple—what has become known as Solomon's Temple—around 960 BC (1 Chr 22:9-10). When it was completed, Solomon prayed before the altar of the Lord and in front of all of Israel (2 Chr 6:12). When he had finished, "Fire came down from heaven and consumed the burnt offerings and sacrifices, and the glory of the Lord filled the house. But the priests could not enter the house of the Lord, for the glory of the Lord filled the house of the Lord. All the Israelites looked on while the fire came down and the glory of the Lord was upon the house, and they fell down upon the pavement with their faces to the earth and worshiped, praising the Lord 'who is so good, whose love endures forever'" (2 Chr 7:1-3). The Temple of Solomon lasted until 587-86 BC when the Babylonians destroyed it, and the Israelites were taken into captivity. The Second Temple was constructed when Cyrus the Great allowed the Israelites to return after the Persians had defeated the Babylonians (Ezr 1:1-4). Completed in 515 BC, it lasted until it was destroyed by the Romans in 70 AD.[9]

A bronze altar was located in the courtyard in front of the Temple for sacrifice. The Holy Place in the Temple held the altar of incense and ten lamp stands (1 Kgs 6:20-21). It also contained a gold plated table for the *lehem ha panim*, which is variously translated as the "Bread of the Presence," "Showbread," "Shewbread," "Perpetual Bread," "Bread of Laying Out," "Bread of Display," or "Bread of Offering," which is the third example of how God was present to the Israelites (Ex 25:30, 35:13, 39:36; Nm 4:7; Mt 12:4; Lk 6:4; Heb 9:2).

God commanded the Israelites to keep the Bread of the Presence "set before me" (Ex 25:30)[10] as a symbol of the covenant (1 Kgs 7:48-49). Each Sabbath, two omers (approximately ten pints) of bran flour were baked into twelve unleavened loaves (one for each tribe) and placed on the gold table in two piles of six loaves each, with two bowls of frankincense between them. The following Sabbath, two priests would approach the table. Each would remove one of the piles, and at the exact moment that the first twelve were removed, two other priests would replace them with twelve more. The four priests gave half of the removed bread to the high priest, and they consumed the rest (Lv 24:5-9).[11]

New Testament

In the New Testament, the theme of God's presence in the Tabernacle, Temple, and bread continues in the person of Jesus of Nazareth. The prologue of the Gospel of John says that "in the beginning was the Word, and the Word was with God, and the Word was God" (1:1). Through the Word, all things came to be. Nothing came to be without him. Life—which was the light of the human race, which shines in the darkness and that has not overcome it, and which enlightens everyone—came to be through him (1:2-10). The Word was in the world, which came to be through him, but it did not know the Word. He came to his own, but his own people did not accept him. To those who accepted him, he gave power to become children of God (1:10-12). As usually translated, the Gospel then says that the Word became flesh "and made his dwelling among us" (1:14). A more literal translation of the original Greek "*skénoó*" would be that the Word "pitched his tent" among us. The first-century audience would understand: just as God pitched his tent in the Tabernacle with the Israelites, God now has pitched his tent in Jesus.

In the next chapter of John, Jesus compares himself to the Temple. As the Passover came near, in the Temple area Jesus found sellers of oxen, sheep, and doves as well as money changers. With a whip of cords, he drove out the oxen, sheep, and their owners, overturned the tables of the money changers, and told those selling the doves to remove the birds and "stop making my Father's house a marketplace" (2:16). Hearing this, Jesus' followers recalled the words of the Psalmist: "Zeal for your house will consume me" (Ps 69:10).[12] The Jews then asked Jesus for a sign that he could show for doing this. "Destroy this temple," he responded to them, "and in three days I will raise it up" (2:19). They pointed out that the Temple had been under continual renovation for the previous forty-six years and were confused at his claim that he would raise it in three days. "But he was speaking about the temple of his body," the author stated (2:21). On the third day after his resurrection, when he was raised from the dead, his disciples "remembered that he had said this, and they came to believe the scripture and the word Jesus had spoken" (2:22).

Throughout the New Testament, Jesus is also described as a new type of the Bread of the Presence. When Caesar Augustus decreed that a census be taken for the entire Roman world, Joseph left Nazareth to return to his hometown "that is called Bethlehem, because he was of the house and family of David, to be enrolled with Mary, his betrothed, who was with child" (Lk 2:4-5). All Christians know this story because of the countless Nativity plays children present every December. Few Christians know, however, that in Hebrew the place where Jesus entered the world, "Bethlehem," means "House of Bread," the first connection between Jesus and bread. After Jesus' birth, Mary "wrapped him in swaddling clothes and laid him in a manger, because there was no room for them in the inn" (Lk 2:7). All Christians know this, too, but few realize that the word "manger," an animal trough, comes from the Latin "*mandere*," which means "to chew." In his infancy narrative, then, Luke establishes the theme of the Eucharist as Jesus' real presence long before his public ministry.

Jesus as the new Bread of the Presence is made explicit in the Bread of Life Discourse. When Jesus was teaching at the synagogue in Capernaum, the crowd, having been fed the previous day with just five barley loaves and two fish, wanted to carry Jesus off and make him king (Jn 6:9-15). They asked for a sign that they may see and believe in him (Jn 6:30). Jesus did not produce a sign, but replied that he himself was the sign, and that "my Father gives you the true bread from heaven" (Jn 6:32). Confused, the crowd murmured among themselves (Jn 6:41-42). Jesus then told them that "I am the living bread that came down from heaven; whoever eats this bread will live forever; and the bread that I will give is my flesh for the life of the world" (Jn 6:51). They then quarreled among themselves, unable to comprehend the meaning of his words. "My flesh is true food," he said, "and my blood is true drink. Whoever eats my flesh and drinks my blood remains in me and I in him" (Jn 6:55-56).

The crowd and many of his own disciples were deeply disturbed by his teaching. Like many down through the centuries who have been unable to assent to his words, they protested: "This saying is hard; who can accept it?" (Jn 6:60). Jesus' words were not simply challenging, but were scandalous because, in demanding that they eat his flesh and drink his blood, he was demanding that they break the dietary restrictions at the very heart of Jewish Law. Jews are permitted to eat some animals, such as those that are both cloven-hoofed and chew the cud (Lv 11:3), but not others, such as those that only chew the cud or have only single hooves (Lv 11:4). Although Jews may eat some animals, they are not permitted to drink blood (Lv 3:17). For many of his disciples, Jesus was demanding too much, so they "returned to their former ways of life and no longer accompanied him" (6:66).

Rather than running after his disciples to tell them that they misheard, misunderstood, or that he was speaking symbolically, Jesus turned to the Twelve—the only ones remaining—and asked, "Do you also want to leave?" (Jn 6:67). Peter replied, "Master, to whom shall we go? You have the words of eternal life. We have come to believe and are convinced that you are the Holy One of God" (Jn 6:68-69). Peter summarized what countless Catholics have believed throughout time: it is impossible to understand the depths of the mystery of Jesus' words, but their gravity prevents many from walking away from the truth that they point toward.

Although they contain slightly different details, all three of the Synoptic Gospels (Mt 26:26-30; Mk 14:22-26; Lk 22:14-20) describe the Last Supper, another important New Testament story demonstrating the Real Presence. For the sake of brevity, we will review only the story told in the Gospel of Matthew.

On the first day of the Feast of the Unleavened Bread, his disciples asked Jesus where he wanted to eat the Passover meal. He told them to leave Bethany and go into Jerusalem. There, they would find a "certain man," and should tell him that Jesus and his disciples would celebrate the Passover because Jesus' appointed time was near (Mt 26:18). They went into the city, found the man, and began preparing for the Passover. During their meal, Jesus took bread, said a prayer blessing God, broke it, and gave it to his disciples, saying "Take and eat; this is my body" (26:26). Then, Jesus took a cup, said another prayer blessing God, and gave it to them, saying "Drink from it all of you, for this is my blood of the covenant, which will be shed on behalf of many for the forgiveness of sins. I tell you, from now on I shall not drink this fruit of the vine until the day when I drink it with you new in the kingdom of my Father" (26:27-29).

The Real Presence of Jesus in the Eucharist throughout the Tradition

One of the earliest (if not *the* earliest) non-canonical Christian texts is the *Didache*, sometimes called *The Teaching of the Lord Through the Twelve Apostles to the Gentiles.*[13] Scholars debate exactly when it was written, but agree that it can be dated as early as the first century, or as late as the beginning of the second century. It even may have been written before the Gospels. Although the *Didache* does not offer an exhaustive teaching on the Eucharist, it provides greater detail about the Eucharist than many other aspects of Christian life. The author instructs the followers of Jesus to come together each Sunday for the confession of sins, to break bread, and to give thanks. The prayer begins with thanks for the chalice, and then for the bread. It includes a petition that, just as the grains of wheat are brought together to make one loaf, "so let your [the Father's] Church be brought together from the ends of the earth into your Kingdom."[14]

Three instructions in the *Didache* indicate that the earliest Christians understood the Eucharist to be more than a symbol. First, it insists that no one should eat or drink of it unless baptized in the name of the Lord because, as Jesus commanded, "Do not give what is sacred to dogs" (Mt 7:6). Second, it says that, after the meal, thanks must be offered because the Father has given bodily food and drink to everyone to enjoy, but also "to us you [the Father] have given spiritual food and drink and eternal life through Jesus, your child."[15] Third, the baptized may not receive if not reconciled to his or her neighbor. By taking the sacred meal while in a dispute with one's neighbor, the sacrificial offering will "be defiled."[16] If the Eucharist were nothing more than bread and wine, the text would not indicate that it is "sacred," that it is "spiritual," and that unworthy reception would cause the sacrifice to be "defiled."

In the early second century, St. Ignatius, the Bishop of Antioch—the first to call the Church "Catholic"—was arrested by the Romans and martyred for his faith. As guards transported him from Asia Minor to Rome for his execution, he wrote letters to seven Christian communities. The most powerful of them was to the community in Rome, who shortly after his arrival would witness his violent end. Ignatius asked them not to interfere, since he understood his impending death to be not the will of the emperor, but the will of God.[17] If, in the drama of his final moments, Ignatius changed his mind and tried to avoid his fate, he begged them to ignore his pleas.[18] Like many Christians after him, he envisioned his martyrdom as an echo of Jesus' own self-giving, and he also envisioned it in a eucharistic key. Just as individual grains of wheat are ground into the one loaf to be changed into Christ and shared for the life of the world, Ignatius saw his own demise as vivifying those watching. "I am God's wheat," he wrote, "and I am being ground by the teeth of wild beasts to make a pure loaf for Christ."[19]

Like the author of the *Didache*, Ignatius claimed that the Eucharist is sacred, but he was even more specific about the nature of the transformed bread and wine. In his plea to the community in Rome, Ignatius expressed his deepest desire to be not for material things, but only for Jesus, who is found in the Eucharist. "I take no delight in corruptible food or the dainties of this life," Ignatius wrote. "What I want is God's bread, which is the flesh of Christ, who came from David's line; and for drink I want his blood: an immortal love feast indeed!"[20] In his letter to the Christian community in Smyrna, Ignatius refuted some heretics who did not believe in the teachings of the Catholic Church.[21] He did not name them, but did call them "wild beasts in human shapes."[22] These heretics, he said, refused to believe that Jesus was truly human, that he suffered, died, and was resurrected, and do not care about widows, orphans, the oppressed, prisoners, or the hungry.

Moreover, they must refrain from receiving the Eucharist because they "refuse to admit that the Eucharist is the flesh of our Savior Jesus Christ, which suffered for our sins and which, in his goodness, the Father raised."[23] Just as the heretics were wrong in their claim that Jesus did not have flesh, they also were wrong that the Eucharist was not Jesus.

During the Middle Ages, the word "transubstantiation" began to be used in theological discourse to describe the transformation of the bread and wine into the body, blood, soul, and divinity of Jesus. Although he did not coin the term (which was first used in an official ecclesial text in 1208 by Pope Innocent III, and again in 1215 at the Fourth Lateran Council),[24] St. Thomas Aquinas is most often associated with it.

Thomas and other theologians borrowed the philosophical categories of "accident" and "substance" from Aristotle, a pre-Christian Greek philosopher, to help explain the conversion of the physical food into spiritual food that the word transubstantiation describes. The accidents of an object, we can say, are "the changeable conditions which do not directly belong to the essence of the thing, but rather answer the question of *how* a thing is."[25] Color, smell, and taste, for example, are accidents of an object. Accidents of the eucharistic bread include the brown color, the brittle texture, and the stale taste. Accidents of the wine include the red color, the fruity smell, and the tart taste.

The substance of an object is "the reality that underlies all the outward appearances or changeable 'accidents' of a thing and gives it its identity."[26] In other words, the substance of an object is its fundamental essence. The substance of the bread is "breadness," and the substance of the wine is "wineness." Transubstantiation, then, describes the conversion of the substance of the bread and the wine (breadness and wineness) into the substance of the body, blood, soul, and divinity of Jesus, while the accidents of the bread and wine (color, texture, taste) remain unchanged.

These philosophical categories may seem abstract and irrelevant, but we all have experienced objects that appear differently than their reality. Many people are colorblind, for example. A shirt that in fact is red may appear green to someone with colorblindness. Automobile drivers are familiar with the statement "objects in the mirror are closer than they appear" at the bottom of the outside mirrors. In the side mirrors a car may appear to be in the distance, but is, in fact, just a few car lengths back. The Eucharist may appear to be bread and wine, but after the consecration it is, in fact, the real presence of Jesus.

Our final witness to the real presence of Jesus in the Eucharist is the Council of Trent (1545-1563), whose most important purpose was to respond to the Protestant Reformation.[27] In the sixteenth century, as the Reformation shattered Christianity, Catholics and Protestants continued to agree on many important theological claims. They agreed, for example, that God is the creator of all things visible and invisible, that Jesus is fully human and fully divine, and that humanity was saved by Jesus. They disagreed, however, on many other issues, such as the authority of the pope, the efficacy of good works, and the need for ordained priests. Arguably, their most important difference was disagreement on the nature of the Eucharist. Not only did Catholics and Protestants disagree about the nature of the Eucharist, but Protestants disagreed among themselves about it—and continue to do so today. Martin Luther, whose posting of his Ninety-Five Theses in 1517 set off the Protestant Reformation, said that the Eucharist "is real bread and real wine, in which Christ's real flesh and real blood are present."[28] Ulrich Zwingli, a Swiss Reformer, claimed that the Eucharist is "that bread which is the symbol of the body of Christ who was put to death for our sakes."[29] John Calvin, another Swiss Reformer, asserted that the body and blood of Jesus are "represented"[30] under the bread and wine. Although the Protestants disagreed among themselves, they all rejected the Catholic teaching of the Real Presence.

The thirteenth session of the Council of Trent issued a decree on the Eucharist. After introductory remarks, the Fathers of the Council affirmed the real presence of Jesus in the Eucharist. "First of all," the decree began, "the holy council [Trent] teaches and openly and plainly professes that after the consecration of bread and wine, our Lord Jesus Christ, true God and true man, is truly, really and substantially contained in the august sacrament of the Holy Eucharist under the appearance of these sensible things."[31] After declaring this, the text asserted that this had been the constant teaching of the Church since the beginning. The decree also reaffirmed the term transubstantiation as "properly and appropriately"[32] articulating the way in which the bread and wine are changed into the body, blood, soul, and divinity of Jesus.

Chapter Two

The Eucharist and Memory

I have only one request to make of you, that you remember me at the altar of the Lord, wherever you may be.

St. Monica

Introduction

The Bread of Life Discourse and the story of the Last Supper that were discussed in the previous chapter are two of the most important biblical passages for understanding the real presence of Jesus in the Eucharist. While the narrative details of the Last Supper are found in the Synoptic Gospels, the description of Jesus' words at the Last Supper comes from St. Paul and predates the first Gospel, the Gospel of Mark, by approximately ten years. In his First Letter to the Corinthians, Paul scolded the community there for their abuse of the *agape* meal (1 Cor 11), the "breaking of the bread" in its initial form before it developed into the Mass (Acts 2:42). He recounted Jesus' words spoken to his followers:

> For I [Paul] received from the Lord what I also handed on to you, that the Lord Jesus, on the night he was handed over, took bread, and, after he had given thanks, broke it and said, "This is my body that is for you. Do this in remembrance of me." In the same way also the cup, after supper, saying, "This cup is the new covenant in my blood. Do this, as often as you drink it, in remembrance of me." For as often as

you eat this bread and drink the cup, you proclaim
the death of the Lord until he comes. (1 Cor 11:23-26)

These verses are saturated with theological significance.

Chapter three will explore what Jesus meant when he said
that his body "is for you," and when he said that this cup "is the
new covenant in my blood." We will restrict our investigation
in this chapter to Jesus' command to do this "in remembrance
of me," which is sometimes translated as "in memory of me."
What does Jesus mean by "do this in memory of me?" Although
Catholics understand that "do this" is a command to repeat
the Last Supper in the Mass, the phrase "in memory of me"
is not as immediately obvious. This chapter will explore the
Christian perspective of memory, what memory has to do with
the Eucharist, and will illustrate the import of the theme of
memory with an example from the life of St. Monica.

A Christian Vision of Memory

Most of us do not take the time or have the inclination to reflect
on the nature of memory. This can lead to a thin understanding of what memory is and what it does. For most, memory is
the mental repository for safekeeping our past events. When
needed, we can retrieve and review our important and precious
experiences, similar to going to a safety-deposit box where our
passports, wills, birth certificates, and family heirlooms are
stored. This mental reclamation can feel like dusting off an an-
tique inherited from our grandparents or getting reacquainted
with a long-lost friend. We lift these memories out of storage and
peruse them, taking "a walk down memory lane," as if retrieving
a memory were little more than watching a television rerun.

The Christian view of memory is much thicker than this.
According to Alexander Schmemann, an Orthodox priest and
theologian, memory is "ultimately inexplicable, mysterious and

even ambiguous."[33] Like the Trinity, the Church, or even the Eucharist itself, memory is ultimately unexplainable and inexhaustible. Having asserted this, Schmemann then claims that "one thing is without doubt: memory is [humanity's] capacity to 'resurrect the past.'"[34] He does not mean that it simply has the ability to bring forth events from our own personal histories—although it certainly does that in its most basic function. Rather, memory has the power to bring the past back from the dead. Memory summons the past and makes it real and actual in the present. It does not make the past "seem" to be present, or "as if" it were present, or "like" it were present. Memory makes the past alive again.

Another way of understanding memory is to look at it from the opposite view: memory transports the present into the past. Prompted by a memory, all the emotions and experiences we felt during a past event—all our failures and successes, all our hopes and fears—rise up in us again in the present and changes us into who we were. Photograph albums, for example, can prompt us to experience memory in this way. On the top shelf in my closet, I have albums of the two years that I spent after college as a Peace Corps Volunteer in the Islamic Republic of Mauritania in West Africa. From time to time, I pull them down and remember the generosity of my host families, the fortitude of my fellow volunteers, and the beauty of the Sahara. But these albums do more than cause mild feelings of nostalgia or regret while I am looking through them. For good and for ill, they take me back to that period of my life again in every part of my being.

Viewing photograph albums can make memories return, but the most powerful sense tied to memory is smell. Countless scents can trigger memories. When I walk into my mother's kitchen on Thanksgiving and smell the same dishes that she made thirty years earlier when I was a child, those moments come rushing back. Sometimes, I cannot even remember what I had for lunch the day before, but the aroma of those familiar foods from holidays past transport me to my childhood again.

The smells bring back once more all the sensations of that day: the scratchiness of my grandpa's sweater as I sat on his lap, the dulcet tones of my uncle's laugh, the corniness of my dad's jokes. Even now, thinking about that meal makes my mouth water; recalling dad's jokes from decades past makes me laugh out loud even now.

Music and Memory

Like photographs and smells, music also summons the past and makes it real and actual in the present—sometimes in unexpected ways. One night while driving a friend's car, I switched on the radio and there came pouring out a song I had never heard before, Eric Church's "Springsteen."

"Springsteen" may seem to be no more than a sugary-sweet ditty about teenage infatuation. But it is, rather, a sophisticated reflection on the nature of memory. The lyrics reveal what memory is and what it does:

To this day when I hear that song
I see you standin' there on that lawn
Discount shades, store bought tan
Flip flops and cut-off jeans

Somewhere between that setting sun
"I'm on Fire" and "Born to Run"
You looked at me and I was done
We were just getting started

I was singin' to you, you were singin' to me
I was so alive, never been more free
Fired up my daddy's lighter and we sang
"Oh-oh-oh-oh, oh-oh"

Stayed there 'til they forced us out
And took the long way to your house
I can still hear the sound
Of you sayin' don't go

When I think about you
I think about 17
I think about my old Jeep
I think about the stars in the sky
Funny how a melody sounds like a memory
Like the soundtrack to a July Saturday night
Springsteen

I bumped into you by happenstance
You probably wouldn't even know who I am
But if I whispered your name I bet
Still be a spark

And back when I was gasoline
And this old tattoo had brand new ink
And we didn't care what your mama would think
'Bout your name on my arms

Baby, is it spring or is it summer?
The guitar sound roll the beat of a drummer
You hear sometimes late at night
On your radio

Even though you're a million miles away
When you hear "Born in the USA."
Do you relive those glory days
So long ago

When you think about me
Do you think about 17?
Do you think about my old Jeep
Think about the stars in the sky?
Funny how a melody sounds like a memory
Like a soundtrack to a July Saturday night

Springsteen
Springsteen

> Funny how a melody sounds like a memory
> Like a soundtrack to a July Saturday night
> Springsteen
>
> Springsteen
> Oh, Springsteen

In the first verse, Church sets the stage of their nascent love. He describes her standing at sunset on a lawn in flip-flop shoes, shorts, tanned, and wearing sunglasses. They were listening to Bruce Springsteen's songs "I'm on Fire," and "Born to Run." The most important part of the verse is not the love, which we later learn vanished about as quickly as it appeared, but how he remembers her. At the beginning, Church sings, "To this day, when I hear that song, I see you standin' there on that lawn." Note that Church claims that "I *see* you" standing on the lawn. He does not say "I seem to recall you there on that lawn," or "I have a wistful recollection of you there on that lawn," or "you had been standing there on that lawn." Rather, he writes "see." He sees her. Right here. Right now. Listening to one of the Springsteen songs in the present moment not only brings back the young woman from the recesses of Church's mind, but she is made present to him—not "as if" he could see her, but in fact, he *does* see her.

The second verse continues this theme. The couple sings to each other, and the love between them, he says, vivifies and liberates him. Free from all cares, they did whatever they wanted: smoked, caused a scene, went home after curfew. Returning to the present, Church sings "I can still hear the sound of you sayin' 'don't go.'" Notice that he says "I can still *hear*" the sound of your voice—not "I can almost hear," or "I think about" it. He says "I can . . . hear." The sound of her voice rings in his ears today exactly as it did the first time.

The fourth verse shifts fully to memory. That young girl is now "a million miles away," a distance in time, not space. As if they were still talking on that lawn, he ponders what causes these memories to rise. Are they brought on by the changing moods of the seasons: the hopefulness of springtime, or the heat of summer? Or, by the music itself: the notes of the guitar or the pulse of the drum in recorded performance that repeats over and over again? Or, by time: the same late hour when their romance blossomed as when the song is played on the radio today? Church doesn't answer his own questions, but asks if her experience is similar. "When you hear 'Born in the U.S.A.,'" he asks, "do you relive those 'Glory Days'?" He asks if the music causes her to "*relive*" the past in the present. He can only ask her this in his mind, as she is not there to share her thoughts with him. It is clear, however, that these songs do make him "relive" those glory days.

In the final chorus, Church asks his former fling about her recollections. What does she recall about their relationship when she was only seventeen? Does she think about his Jeep? Does she think about the stars they saw as they took the long way home? Church repeats the refrain at the end of each verse: "Funny how a melody sounds like a memory. Like a soundtrack to a July Saturday night. Springsteen." On the surface, Church is pointing to the "funny" repetition of the "me" sound in both "*me*lody," and "*me*mory." On a deeper level, he is pointing to the power of a song's melody to summon a personal memory and make it real in the present moment.

The title of this song is important. He did not name it after his adolescent love, but after Bruce Springsteen, shifting our focus from the girl to memory. The Springsteen songs act as a time machine, if you will, transporting his past relationship into the present. Whatever they were doing on that July night— holding hands, kissing, telling each other their most intimate secrets—Church "sees," "hears," and "relives," it all over again.

Of course, this is true not only for the character in Church's song, but for all of us. We all have songs, books, movies, or pieces of clothing that do this to us and for us. Sometimes the memories are sweet, at other times painful, sometimes both at the same time. Many events in my own past are tied to songs. The summer during high school I spent living with my aunt and uncle in Myrtle Beach comes rushing back to me every time I hear the Counting Crows' "Round Here." Fleetwood Mac's "Never Going Back Again" conjures memories of my time in Africa. Pink's "Raise Your Glass," which was played at the reception-turned-dance-party after my RCIA group received the Sacrament of Reconciliation for the first time just before we all came into full communion with the Catholic Church, makes me relive that night. Regardless of our unique events, emotions, or circumstances, this mysterious power of memory touches us all.

The Eucharist and Memory

Sensory experiences like looking at a photograph album or stepping into mom's kitchen can make the past present. But beyond what the senses can do, it is the liturgy that has the most powerful ability to collapse time. In *Models of the Eucharist*, liturgist Msgr. Kevin Irwin shows the power of liturgy to make present not just the personal events of our own lives, but to make present the most important events of all, the "saving events" in history.[35] In "making memory," he says, "what we proclaim and experience through liturgical actions reiterates and deepens among us what God did (not only 'said') once for all in saving history."[36] In the liturgy, it is not we who remember. That would be impossible since, in the case of the Last Supper, we were not at the table two thousand years ago. Rather, by these liturgical actions "God does something. God acts on our behalf. Through liturgical memorial we are drawn into God's eternal act of salvation, re-creation, and redemption."[37] By "doing something" on our behalf, God opens up the possibility for us to "remember" the past. But liturgy takes us one step further than sensory experiences because it does more than simply make the past present to us. Through liturgy, we who were not present at the original event "share in the saving events that occurred in history but that cannot be confined to history (in the sense of chronology). The liturgical notion of making memory is *doing* and participating in *an act of memory* in which the very same events of history that are called 'saving' are actualized, that is, realized, and experienced once again through the present liturgy. These 'saving' events are so extraordinary that they transcend the time and place in which they originally took place."[38] In other words, the liturgy now allows us to participate in God's past salvific work.

At the Last Supper, Jesus commanded his followers to "do this in memory of me." The "do this," as mentioned earlier, was his command to repeat the Last Supper in the Eucharist down through the centuries. His command "in memory of me" is now becoming clearer. The central meaning of Jesus' directive is that receiving the Eucharist makes actual to us today the entire saving event of Jesus' incarnation, birth, life, passion, death, and resurrection. In other words, as St. John Paul II explained, in the Eucharist Jesus "brought about a mysterious 'oneness in time' between that *Triduum* and the passage of the centuries"[39] so that "each member of the faithful can thus take part in it and inexhaustibly gain its fruits."[40]

Through memory, the past is not only resurrected in the present, but the present is brought to the past. Catholic theologian Louis Bouyer suggests that this understanding of memory is not an expression of wish fulfillment, or psychological delusion, as many today might suspect, and so may dismiss it. "It in no way means a subjective, human psychological act of returning to the past," Bouyer wrote, "but an objective reality destined to make some thing or some one perpetually present before God and for God himself."[41] In celebrating and receiving the Eucharist at the hands of the priest, we in the twenty-first century are taken to the Jesus event in the first century.[42] In a very real way, the Eucharist allows us to be present in the

Upper Room with Jesus and his disciples—we receive Christ's body and blood along with those who gathered around the table with him (Mt 26:26-29).[43]

The Eucharist, Memory, and St. Monica

The account in *The Confessions* of the death of St. Monica—the mother of one of the most important theologians in the history of Christianity, St. Augustine, the "Doctor of Grace"—vividly brings to life this integration of the Eucharist and memory.[44] Augustine, Monica, and their company were attempting to return to North Africa from Italy not long after St. Ambrose of Milan had baptized Augustine. They were delayed outside of Rome, in Ostia, because of political and military unrest. Monica fell ill, possibly of malaria.[45] Earlier in her life, she had told Augustine and his brother, Navigius, that she wanted to be buried in Thagaste next to her husband, Patricius. Now on her deathbed, she told her sons to bury her there in Italy. Navigius, attempting to cheer her up, told her that he hoped that she would be buried in her home soil, not in a foreign land. This did not please her, however, and she admonished him for even having such a thought. She commanded her sons to "bury my body anywhere you like. Let no anxiety about this disturb you. I have only one request to make of you, that you remember me at the altar of the Lord, wherever you may be."[46]

Monica's statement overflows with meaning. Telling her sons that they may "bury my body anywhere you like" does not mean that she believed the body to be insignificant, a shell, or, even worse, a prison for the soul. Many religions and philosophies in late antiquity held the view that once the soul has left the body, the body could be discarded like skin shed from a snake. Monica did not believe this. For her, the body is good because it is created by God and will be resurrected on the last day (1 Cor 15:36-58). So, telling her sons that they may bury her wherever they wished was not a rejection of the body. Rather, she meant that the geographic location of her final resting place is ultimately meaningless. It did not matter whether her body was buried in Italy or in North Africa. For "nothing," as she later said, "is distant from God."[47]

The second consequential part of Monica's statement is that she had "only one request to make of you, that you remember me at the altar of the Lord, wherever you may be." When we imagine how we will die, who will surround us on our deathbed, what we will feel in those final moments, and what our last words will be, most of us hope that we will die in bed at home with our loved ones surrounding us. For her to have "only one" request underscores the importance of her desire. There is nothing that she would consider more important than for her children to "remember" her after she dies. This is, of course, because Monica understood everything we have discussed in this chapter about memory. When her children remember her, Monica will not be present to them in a superficial or vague manner. She will be present to them fully.

She did not want her children just to remember her when they listen to music, or on specific occasions, such as her birthday, or on the anniversary of the day that she died. She specifically requested that they remember her "at the altar of the Lord" because for her the altar "is the true locus of memory."[48] The next chapter will discuss the significance of the altar for Jews as the place where the sacrifices were made in the Temple, and for Catholics, where the sacrifice of Jesus is re-presented in the Eucharist today. It is enough to know now that Monica was requesting that they remember her when they receive the Eucharist. In other words, she asked that her children remember her at the same moment that Jesus is present to them in the Eucharist. In that moment Monica, her children, and Jesus come together in a mystical and sacramental communion that words cannot convey.

The Eucharist and Sacrifice

The cup of blessing that we bless, is it not a participation in the blood of Christ?

The bread that we break, is it not a participation in the body of Christ?

St. Paul

Introduction

Jesus died on the cross for the sins of humanity. Although this undoubtedly is a fundamental Christian claim, on the surface it makes little sense. If aliens were to come from outer space and hear this statement, would they make any obvious connection between the execution of an obscure rabbi and the expiation of all human sins? Why did Jesus die? Why on a cross? What does his death have to do with the sins of humanity? The short answer to these questions is that his death on the cross was a sacrifice. This, too, would make little sense to these extraterrestrials because understanding fully what sacrifice means requires knowledge of the first-century Jewish context of sacrifice, temple, and priesthood. This chapter will unpack the logic of sacrifice, why Jesus' death was sacrificial, and how the Eucharist is the primary means whereby Catholics today are able to receive the fruits of that sacrifice.

Sacrifice

Colloquially, "sacrifice" has come to mean little more than "giving something up," like abstaining from chocolate during Lent, or bunting to advance a runner in baseball. Theologically, sacrifice has a much richer, deeper, and more textured definition. It is difficult to encapsulate that richness in a few sentences because if, as the saying goes, "a picture is worth a thousand words," then a ritual act such as a sacrifice must be worth ten million words.

Etymologically, the word "sacrifice" comes from two Latin words: "*sacer*," which means "holy," and "*facere*," which means "to make."[49] Sacrifice, in its most basic understanding, is "to make holy," or "to set apart."[50] In the Jewish milieu of Jesus' time, sacrifice meant this and more. The Old Testament Hebrew word for sacrifice is "*korban*." Joshua Berman points out that *korban* "comes from the [Hebrew] root *k.r.v.*, meaning 'close.' The word *korban* literally means 'that which has been brought close,' and it refers to the sacrifice of something that enters into God's presence in the Sanctuary. To offer a sacrifice is termed *le-hakriv korban*—literally, 'to bring the sacrifice close.'"[51]

For the Israelites, *korban* had multiple layers of meaning. First, it is an acknowledgement that God is Lord over all creation. This recognition occurs when part of what already belongs to God is offered in return. Second, it was an act of thanksgiving. Third, it was the primary way that God and Israel established covenants (Ps 50:5), permanent agreements establishing a relationship between two people, or groups of people. For example, at the base of Mt. Sinai, God sealed a covenant with Moses and the Israelites. Moses built an altar and sacrificed bulls. He collected the blood of the sacrificed animals in bowls and splashed half on the Israelites and the other half on an altar that represented the Lord (Ex 24:1-11).[52] Positively, the blood symbolized the establishment of an unbreakable relationship. Negatively, the slaughter of animals symbolized the death that would result if the covenant were transgressed.[53] Fourth, *korban* was an act of repentance for the sins the Israelites had committed.[54]

The Christian grasp of the meaning of sacrifice is rooted in this Jewish understanding. In *The Living Bread*, the Trappist spiritual writer Thomas Merton explained the goals of sacrifice using Jesus' own words from the Gospel of John. Just before his arrest in the Garden of Gethsemane, Jesus prayed: "Father, glorify thy Son, that thy Son may glorify thee.... I am glorified in them (whom thou hast given me) ... For them do I sanctify myself that they may be sanctified in truth.... And the glory which Thou hast given me I have given them; that they may be one as we also are one ... I will that where I am they also may be, that they may see my glory" (Jn 17:1, 10, 19, 22, 24).[55] For Merton, Jesus' words point to four ends of sacrifice. First, it gives "infinite glory to God," its most important end; second, it gives God "a perfect return of praise and thanksgiving for all His goodness to men"; third, it offers God "a worthy propitiation for all our sins"; finally, it obtains "all the temporal and spiritual aids which we need in order to carry out His will on earth and come to union with Him in heaven."[56] What Merton explains remains at the heart of the Christian understanding today. In harmony with the Jewish tradition, Jesus saw his own impending passion and death as the culmination of Jewish sacrifice, as this chapter will spell out.

Sacrifice in the Old Testament

Sacrifice is at the heart of the Old Testament. In Genesis, Cain and Abel both made sacrifices to God. Cain, a tiller of the ground, brought the Lord an offering from the fruit of the earth while Abel, a herder, brought the fatty portion of the firstlings of his flock. The Lord looked with favor on Abel and his offering, but not on Cain and his. Genesis does not specify why Cain's was rejected, only that God said "If you act rightly, you will be accepted," implying that Cain's offering was improper in some way.

A second Old Testament example is the *Akedah*, the binding of Isaac, one of the most perplexing stories in the Bible. God tested Abraham by commanding him to take Isaac to the land of Moriah and sacrifice him as a burnt offering. Without hesitation or protest, Abraham saddled his donkey and took his son, two servants, and wood for the offering. After three days, Abraham left the donkey and the two servants. He placed the wood on Isaac's back and carried the knife and the fire. Isaac asked his father where they would find a sheep for the offering. The text does not offer a commentary about Abraham's state of mind when Isaac asked this question. Was he distraught? Was he angry? Was he confident that God would intervene? All we know is that he responded that "God will provide the sheep for the burnt offering." When they arrived, Abraham built an altar and placed the wood on it. Binding Isaac, he placed him on the altar. As Abraham poised to slice Isaac's throat—as hauntingly portrayed by Caravaggio in his painting *Sacrifice of Isaac*—an angel of the Lord stopped him. He then saw a ram caught in a thicket. In place of his son, he sacrificed the ram. The angel of the Lord spoke again, saying that because Abraham did not withhold Isaac, the Lord repeated his promise to make Abraham's descendants as numerous as the stars in the sky and the sands on the shore. The Lord also promised that they would vanquish their enemies, and in his descendants all the nations of earth will find blessing (Gn 22:1-19).

The most important sacrifice in Jewish life was (and is) the Passover before the Israelites fled Egypt, and the yearly commemoration of that pivotal moment in the life of the Israelite community. When Moses (begrudgingly) returned to Egypt at the prompting of I AM WHO I AM to free the Israelites from slavery (Ex 3:7-4:9), the Lord sent down ten plagues on Egypt (Ex 7:14 – 11:10) because Pharaoh would not let the Israelites go (Ex 7:13). The tenth plague is the most shocking (Ex 11:1-10). Around midnight the Lord struck down every firstborn in all of Egypt, including Pharaoh's son (Ex 12:29-30).

The firstborn of the Israelites were spared because Moses had instructed the elders to slaughter lambs, drain their blood into basins, dip hyssop into the blood, and brush it on the lintel (support beam across the top of the door) and the two doorposts of their homes. The Lord then would see the blood and "pass over" the door and would not allow "the destroyer" to enter into the Israelite houses to kill their firstborn (Ex 12:21-28). After this final plague, Pharaoh ordered the Israelites to leave Egypt with their flocks and herds and demanded that Moses bless him (Ex 12:30).

This liberation was so important for the Israelites that the Lord commanded them to celebrate the Passover yearly (Ex 12:14), beginning on the tenth day of the month of Nisan (around March/April). Each house was to procure a year-old male lamb without blemish. On the fourteenth day, at twilight, the entire community was to slaughter the lambs and each household was to apply some of the blood to the lintel and doorposts. That same night, with loins girt, feet shod with sandals, and staff in hand, the people were to eat the roasted meat, with unleavened bread and bitter herbs. None of the bones were to be broken (Ex 12:43-49). Then, for seven days, the Israelites were to eat bread in homes clean of all leaven in memory of those who, when they fled from Egypt, ate unleavened bread because there was not enough time for bread to rise (Ex 12:39). When children would inquire about the meaning of it all, the parents were to respond, "It is the Passover sacrifice for the Lord, who passed over the houses of the Israelites in Egypt; when he struck down the Egyptians, he delivered our houses" (Ex 12:27).

Consuming the meat of the lamb is the heart of the sacrifice. Scott Hahn notes the centrality of such consumption to the existence of the Jewish people: "That [Passover] was the act

that renewed the covenant. That was the act that constituted
Israel as a nation. That was the act by which individual Jews
knew communion with one another and with God. "[57] This
particular sacrifice, more than any other, is the very event that
allowed—and still allows—Jewish life to continue.

Originally, individuals such as Cain, Abel, Noah, and
Abraham offered their own sacrifices. Over time, the Mosaic
Law permitted only priests to offer sacrifices and reserved
them to the Temple alone (Dt 12:10-14). Temple priests—like
Catholic priests today—represent the community as media-
tors between God and humanity: "The people offer sacrifice
together *through* the hands of the priest. In every ritual sacrifice, therefore, we can distinguish a ministerial priest who
offers on behalf of the community and the people as a whole
who offer through him."[58] Israelite priests were different from
Catholic priests in several key respects, however. Unlike their
counterparts, who have discerned and responded to God's call
to be ordained, Israelite priests were born into the priesthood.

After the Israelites had been liberated, the Lord granted
priestly authority to Aaron the Levite (the brother of Moses)
and his sons (Ex 4:14; 28:1); indeed, Aaron became the first high
priest (Ex 35-40). When the Israelites committed idolatry by
worshiping the molten calf (Ex 32: 1-6), Moses punished them
by grinding the idol into powder, throwing it in the stream
that flowed down Sinai (Dt 9:21), and forcing the Israelites
to drink it (Ex 32: 19-20). When he cried out that whoever
was "for the Lord" should rally to him (Ex 32:26), only the
Levites—the descendants of Levi, one of the twelve sons of
Jacob (Israel)—responded. Moses ordered them to "kill your
brothers, your friends, your neighbors" (Ex 32:27); the Levites
killed approximately three thousand (Ex 32:28). Because they
alone responded to Moses, they were installed as priests for
the Lord (Ex 32:29) to assist Aaron and his sons (Nm 3:1-39).

Once the Temple had been built in Jerusalem, each morning
and evening priests sacrificed there a one-year-old lamb for the

sins of all Israel (Ex 29:38-42).[59] Echoing the requirement for
the Passover feast, these animals had to be without blemish.[60]
A variety of "clean" animals were sacrificed in the Temple,
mainly oxen, sheep, and goats. Some birds—turtledoves and
pigeons—also could be substituted, but only if the offeror were
poor (Lv 11:1-47; Dt 14:1-21). Some food offerings usually accompanied an animal sacrifice, including wine, cereal offerings
sprinkled with salt (Lv 2:13), and oil. Fragrant incense, such as
frankincense, was required on a daily basis (Ex 30:7-8).

To understand the death of Jesus as a sacrifice it is crucial to
understand the five different sacrificial offerings at the Temple.[61]
The Lord told Moses how each should be offered (Lv 1:1-2).
The first, the burnt offering, was an unblemished male animal. The offeror pressed his hand on the head of the animal so
that "it may be acceptable to make atonement for the one who
offers it." In Hebrew, this laying of hands is called *semikhah*,
which means "to lean." When "leaning," the one offering the
sacrifice transferred his weight (of sins) to the animal. "The
owner leans on his designated animal, conferring an ailment
of his identity onto it. It is no coincidence that the *Halakhah*
[Jewish Law] calls for the owner to lean on the animal with
both hands, with all his force. When the owner leans on the
animal with the full force of his weight, he is supported by the
animal alone. It is this rite that manifests the notion that the
animal stands in the place of the owner himself."[62] After the
"weight" of sin had been transferred to the animal, the priests
ritually drained its blood, slaughtered it, then splashed its
blood on the sides of the altar.

Blood—then as now—is charged with meaning that
transcends poetic metaphor. Although blood stains whatever it touches, it was viewed as a spiritual cleansing agent.
Moreover, it

> symbolizes a person's soul—his essence, his inner-
> most identity and being. Blood rites, then, can be seen

as uniquely evocative symbols of commitment and
devotion. . . . When someone commits his devotion
to another, he commits his entire being—he defines
his very essence in terms of the object of his devotion.
To commit one's devotion, then, is to precipitate a
transformation of the soul. No symbol could more
vividly reflect this transformation of the soul than
the blood, the substance that symbolizes the soul.[63]

Through the blood of the sacrifice, the offeror commits his
entire self to the Lord. After the blood was spread on the
sides of the altar, the animal was skinned and its flesh, inner
organs, head, and shanks were placed atop burning embers
on the altar. The aroma of the burning sacrifice ascended to
the Lord to appease him. No part of the burnt offering was
eaten (Lv 1:3-17; 6:1-6).

The second, the cereal offering, accompanied animal sacrifices. Bran flour or bran cakes were presented to the Aaronic
priests (the descendants of Aaron). The bran flour was covered
in oil, and frankincense was put over it. Unleavened cakes of
bran flour mixed with oil or unleavened wafers spread with
oil were to be baked, fried on a griddle, or cooked in a pan.
The cereal offering was broken into pieces, oil was poured over
it, and was salted, symbolizing friendship and social alliance
(Mk 9:49-50; Col 4:6). The priests burned some of the offering
on the altar as "a sweet-smelling oblation to the Lord," taking
the rest for themselves to eat (Lv 2:1-16; 6:7-11).

The third, the peace offering, was a festive repast intended
to strengthen the covenantal bond between the offeror and
the Lord. As in the burnt offering, the animal could have no
blemish, but could be either a male or a female. The offeror
placed his hand on the animal's head, then the priests slaughtered the animal and splashed its blood on all sides of the
altar. The fatty portions and kidneys were burnt on the altar,
the brisket and the right leg were given to the priests, and the
rest was returned to be eaten on the same day it was offered

(Dt 27:7). The meat was to be consumed; but if anything unclean touched it, it had to be burned. If someone unclean were to eat the meat, that person was to be cut off from the community (Lv 3:1-17; 7:11-36).

The fourth, the sin offering, was made to atone for unintentionally breaking the Lord's prohibitions. The type of animal varied, depending upon the social status of the offeror. If the offeror were the entire Israelite people or a priest, it would be an unblemished bull; if the offeror were a leader of a tribe, an unblemished male goat; if the offeror were someone of undistinguished social rank, a female kid or lamb; or, if the offeror were poor, two turtledoves or pigeons. Like the burnt and peace offerings, after the offeror pressed his hand on the animal it was drained of its blood and slaughtered. Some of the blood was sprinkled seven times toward the veil of the sanctuary and spread on the horns of the altar, while the rest was poured out at the base of the altar, on which the fatty portions and kidneys were burnt. The priests took some of the meat to be eaten, and the rest of the animal was taken outside of the city to a ritually pure place to be burned (Lv 4:1-5:13; 6:17-23).

The fifth, the guilt offering, was an unblemished ram. After it was slaughtered, its blood was splashed on the sides of the altar and the fatty portions, kidneys, and the lobe of the liver were burned on the altar. The priests were permitted to eat the remaining meat. The motives for this offering varied. Someone who unintentionally used the Lord's sacred objects incorrectly needed to restore the sacred objects, offer the ram, and give one-fifth of its value to the priests. Someone who inadvertently violated the Lord's commands would offer a ram once the transgression was realized. Someone who defrauded or deceived a neighbor needed to remedy the injustice, offer a ram, and give one-fifth of its value to the neighbor (Lv 5:14-26; 7:1-10).

Sacrifice and Jesus

A basic grasp of Jewish thought, history, and practice of the cult of sacrifice prepares us to turn our attention to the New Testament. The earliest followers of Jesus recognized and described the connections between sacrifice and, as John the Baptist called him, "the Lamb of God who takes away the sin of the world" (Jn 1:29). Unfortunately, no single text makes those connections in an organized and systematic fashion; rather, they are peppered throughout the twenty-seven books of the New Testament.

The New Testament authors were keen to demonstrate how the Old and New Testaments are related. As Augustine articulated that connection, "The New Testament is hidden in the Old and the Old is made manifest in the New."[64] More specifically, Christians understand that even though the name "Jesus" is not found there, the Old Testament foreshadows his incarnation in numerous ways. Benedict XVI has asserted that "the New Testament itself claims to be consistent with the Old and proclaims that in the mystery of the life, death and resurrection of Christ the sacred Scriptures of the Jewish people have found their perfect fulfilment."[65]

The Old Testament anticipates Jesus and his sacrifice in the Book of Isaiah, particularly the part concerning the "Suffering Servant" (52:13-53:12). The fourth of four "Servant Songs" in Isaiah (40-55) describe a mysterious figure who was God's "chosen one with whom I am pleased. Upon him I have put my spirit" (42:1). In the first "Servant Song," God calls the Servant for his mission to "establish justice on earth" (42:1-9). In the second, the Servant affirms God's call and his mission to restore the Israelites and be the light to the nations (49:1-7). In the third, the Servant describes the physical tortures he has endured, and his reliance on God (50:4-11). The fourth (52:13 – 53:12) details the full horrors that the Servant experienced, including his unjust end: "He was given a grave among the

wicked, a burial place with evildoers, though he had done
no wrong, nor was deceit found in his mouth" (53:9). Most
importantly for our purposes, this fourth "Servant Song" is
infused with images of the Servant being offered as a sacrificial
guilt offering (53:10). Here are some of the key passages from
the fourth "Servant Song," and the corresponding passages
from the New Testament that make the connection between
the Servant and Jesus:

- **Is 53:4** "Yet it was our pain that he bore, our sufferings
  he endured. We thought of him as stricken, struck
  down by God and afflicted."

- **Mt 8:17** ". . . to fulfill what had been said by Isaiah the
  prophet: 'He took away our infirmities and bore our
  diseases.'"

- **Is 53:5** "But he was pierced for our sins, crushed for
  our iniquity. He bore the punishment that makes us
  whole, by his wounds we were healed."

- **Is 53:11** "Because of his anguish he shall see the light;
  because of his knowledge he shall be content; My servant, the just one, shall justify the many, their iniquity
  he shall bear."

- **1 Pt 2:24** "He himself bore our sins in his body upon
  the cross, so that, free from sin, we might live for righteousness. By his wounds you have been healed."

- **Is 53:7-8** "Though harshly treated, he submitted and
  did not open his mouth; Like a lamb led to slaughter
  or a sheep silent before shearers, he did not open his
  mouth. Seized and condemned, he was taken away.
  Who would have thought any more of his destiny? For
  he was cut off from the land of the living, struck for
  the sins of his people."

- **Acts 8:32-33** "This was the scripture passage he [the Ethiopian whom Philip met] was reading: 'Like a sheep he was led to the slaughter, and as a lamb before its shearer is silent, so he opened not his mouth. In [his] humiliation justice was denied him. Who will tell of his posterity? For his life is taken from the earth.'"

- **Is 53:12** "Therefore I will give him his portion among the many, and he shall divide the spoils with the mighty, because he surrendered himself to death, was counted among the transgressors, bore the sins of many, and interceded for the transgressors."

- **Rom 4:25** "[Jesus] who was handed over for our transgressions and was raised for our justification."

- **Heb 9:28** "So also Christ, offered once to take away the sins of many, will appear a second time, not to take away sin but to bring salvation to those who eagerly await him."

Jesus' earliest followers saw the Suffering Servant in Jesus himself and saw him "pierced for our sins" (Is 53:5) in the crucifixion.

Jesus' sacrifice—his passion and death on the cross—not only fulfilled what Isaiah prophesied concerning the Suffering Servant, but Christians understand it also as *the* Passover celebration. Earlier in this chapter, we saw that Moses commanded the elders to dip hyssop in the blood of the lamb and to brush it on their lintels and doorposts (Ex 12:21-23). In the Gospel of John, hyssop reappears at the moment of Jesus' death: "After this, aware that everything was now finished, in order that the scripture might be fulfilled, Jesus said, 'I thirst.' There was a vessel filled with common wine. So they put a sponge soaked in wine on a sprig of hyssop and put it in his mouth. When Jesus had taken the wine, he said, 'It is finished.'" (19:28-30).

Just as the hyssop marked the salvation of the Israelites' first-born from death, the hyssop later marked the salvation of all humanity from death through Jesus on the cross.

We also saw earlier that an essential requirement of the Passover sacrifice is that the animal be unblemished—specifically, none of its bones may be broken (Ex 12:43-49). During the crucifixion, the Jews asked Pilate to speed the death of those crucified so that the bodies would not remain on the cross during the Sabbath. The soldiers broke the legs of the two crucified with Jesus but did not need to break his legs as he was already dead. Instead, one of the soldiers thrust a lance into his side. Blood and water flowed forth (19:31-37). John explicitly connects Jesus with the Passover: "This happened so that the scripture passage might be fulfilled: 'not a bone of it will be broken'" (19:36). The First Letter of Peter also echoes this: "If you invoke as Father him who judges impartially according to each one's works, conduct yourselves with reverence during the time of your sojourning, realizing that you were ransomed from your futile conduct, handed on by your ancestors, not with perishable things like silver or gold, but with the precious blood of Christ as of a spotless unblemished lamb" (1:17-19).

The Gospel of John is one of the most important texts for understanding Jesus as sacrificial victim. Just before he was crucified, Jesus was brought to Pilate when "it was preparation day for Passover, and it was about noon" (Jn 19:14). The detail that it was "about noon" (sometimes translated as "about the sixth hour") during the preparation day for Passover is significant. John is indicating that Jesus was a sacrificial victim because at the same time on the same day of his crucifixion, the priests at the Temple were beginning to slaughter the lambs for the Passover feast.

The crucifixion also echoes the paschal slaughter in the Temple. The Mishnah, the codified collection of Jewish oral laws, recounts that priests at the Temple first would drain the lamb of its blood, and then pierce the lamb's shoulders with a wooden stave in order to suspend and skin it. Then, a piece of pomegranate wood would be plunged from its mouth to its anus. The Talmudic scholar Joseph Tabory concludes that "in Jerusalem the Jewish paschal lamb was offered in a manner which resembled a crucifixion."[66] Even though the Temple had been destroyed for almost a hundred years, in the second-century *Dialogue with Trypho*, the Christian apologist Justin Martyr recounted that "the lamb, while being roasted, resembles the figure of the cross, for one spit transfixes it [the lamb] horizontally from the lower parts up to the head, and another pierces it across the back and holds it up by its forelegs."[67] Though the crucifixion was a Roman form of torture and execution, that same image was witnessed by Jews in countless lambs "crucified" at the Temple for Passover.

The Letter to the Hebrews, even more explicitly than John, points to Jesus as sacrificial victim. It points out the limits of the Temple animal sacrifices because they needed to be repeated (10:1-2). Christ's sacrifice, alternatively, was offered only once, and never repeated: "Every priest stands daily at his ministry, offering frequently those same sacrifices that can never take away sins. But this one [Jesus] offered one sacrifice for sins, and took his seat forever at the right hand of God; now he waits until his enemies are made his footstool" (Heb 10:11-14). Jesus' sacrifice never needed to be repeated because, as high priest, Jesus was different from other priests, who were flawed and sinful. As both human and divine, Jesus was different; he has "no need, as did the high priests, to offer sacrifice day after day, first for his own sins and then for those of the people; he did that once for all when he offered himself. For the law appoints men subject to weakness to be high priests, but the word of the oath, which was taken after the law appoints a son, who has been made perfect forever" (7:26-28). Moreover, Jesus negated animal sacrifices because the Father did not desire them (Ps 40:7-9; 10:5-7). Jesus, rather, came to do the will of the Father

(Heb 10:8-9) by which humanity has been consecrated by the body of Jesus himself (Heb 10:10).

The crucifixion itself also points to the sacrificial elements of Jesus' death. First, Jesus was taken to the Place of the Skull (Golgotha) outside of Jerusalem (Jn 19:17-20). One requirement of the sin offering at the Temple, as discussed earlier, was that some of the slaughtered meat be given to the priests, but the rest be taken outside of the city (and burned). Second, like all sacrificed animals, Jesus was drained of his blood (Jn 19:34)—blood that "cleanses us from all sin" (1 Jn 1:7). Third, although he was not skinned like the animals burnt on the altar, he was stripped of his clothes and his body scourged (Mt 27:29). Taken together, these details reveal more clearly the sacrificial dimension of Christ's death.

The Eucharist and Sacrifice

Paired with the cross, the Last Supper—the moment when Jesus instituted the Eucharist, the means by which "he has made present his sacrifice everywhere day after day"[68]—is undoubtedly the center of the sacrificial dimension of Jesus' life.[69] In many ways, this meal was a typical Jewish Passover celebration, but unexpected dimensions of the ritual were also added.[70] Most importantly for our purposes, Jesus transformed the meaning of the already meaningful bread and wine. Because the words are repeated at every Mass, Catholics may be familiar with Jesus' commands at the Last Supper but may miss the depth of their power. During the meal, Jesus took the bread, broke it, and gave it to his followers, saying "This is my body, which will be given for you" (Lk 22:19). Jesus' statement that his body "will be given for you" echoes the prophet Isaiah: "It was the Lord's will to crush him [the Suffering Servant] with pain. By making his life an offering for sin,[71] he shall see his offspring, shall enlighten his days, and the Lord's will shall be accomplished through him" (Is 53:10). Jesus' followers surely recognized how both Jesus and the Suffering Servant gave their bodies for others.

Jesus then took the cup and said, "Drink from it, all of you, for this is my blood of the covenant, which will be shed [that is, poured out] on behalf of many for the forgiveness of sins." (Mt 26:27-28).[72] Jesus' followers also would have recognized the four sacrificial elements of this statement. First, Jesus' claim that his blood is the "blood of the covenant" harkens back to what we saw earlier when Moses, at the foot of Sinai, built an altar, collected the blood of the sacrificed bulls in bowls, and splashed half of the blood on the Israelites and the other half on the altar that represented the Lord (Ex 24:1-11). As Moses did this he said, "This is the blood of the covenant which the Lord has made with you according to all these words" (Ex 24:8).

Second, Jesus' claim that his blood was "shed" or "poured out" refers back to the blood of the sacrificial animals in the Temple. Earlier, we saw that, after the animal was slaughtered for the sin offering, some of the blood was sprinkled seven times toward the veil of the sanctuary and spread on the horns of the altar, while the rest was poured out at the base of the altar for burnt offerings. Third, Jesus' claim again alludes to the Suffering Servant. Just as the Suffering Servant "poured out" his life "unto death" (Is 53:12),[73] Jesus "poured out" his blood on behalf of many for the forgiveness of sins. Fourth, the Suffering Servant shall "justify the many" (Is 53:11), and bear "the sins of many" (53:13); Jesus' blood was poured out "on behalf of many." Jesus clearly intended that he, the Last Supper, the Eucharist, and the cross be understood as an integrated whole.

The Eucharist instituted at the Last Supper and now celebrated daily are the same sacrifice. In his *Homilies on the Letter to the Hebrews*, St. John Chrysostom preached that the cross and Eucharist are one, affirming that "we always offer the same Lamb, not one now and another tomorrow, but always the same one, so that the sacrifice is one. . . . As then while offered in many places, He is one body and not many bodies; so also [he is] one sacrifice. He is our High Priest, who offered the sacrifice that cleanses us."[74] The Eucharist, in other words, is the sacramental *re*-presentation of Christ's sacrifice on the cross—not a representation of the cross.[75] The Eucharist does not represent the sacrifice—that is, it does not "stand in" for the sacrifice in the way that a lawyer "stands in" for a client. Rather, it re-presents the sacrifice in an entirely different manner. As Bishop Barron has described it, the Eucharist "recapitulates" the first century sacrifice, and brings "the power of the cross to bear in the present."[76] John Paul II, moreover, said that the Eucharist is the cross "perpetuated down the ages,"[77] even, according to the Council of Trent, "to the end of the world."[78] In re-presenting the sacrifice, the Eucharist perpetuates and makes present that sacrifice today because "the sacrifice of Christ and the sacrifice of the Eucharist are one single sacrifice."[79]

When Catholics receive the Eucharist, they participate in this re-presented sacrifice of the cross. Participation in sacrifice through a meal was a common practice across many religions throughout the ancient world. It was not unique to the early followers of Jesus. Paul knew this and understood the danger that the community in Corinth faced if they participated in both pagan sacrifice and the sacrifice of the cross. He warned them against eating meat sacrificed to pagan idols because those idols were demons. By eating that sacrificed meat, the Corinthians would participate in something demonic (1 Cor 10:19-20).

Paul knew that Jews also shared this same sense of participation: "Look at Israel according to the flesh; are not those who eat the sacrifices [from the Temple] participants in the altar?" (1 Cor 10:18). For Jews, the altar represented the Lord.[80] Eating and drinking the consecrated bread and wine, Paul said, is even more profound than eating sacrificed animals, whether from pagan shrines or from the Temple. Paul asked, "The cup of blessing that we bless, is it not a participation in the blood of Christ? The bread that we break, is it not a participation in the body of Christ?" (1 Cor 10:16). He pointed out to the community in Corinth the peril of participating in both pagan sacrifices and the sacrifice of Christ: "You cannot drink the cup of the Lord and also the cup of demons. You cannot partake of the table of the Lord and of the table of demons. Or are we provoking the Lord to jealous anger? Are we stronger than he?" (1 Cor 10:21-22). Participating in both the table of the Lord and the table of demons would break the first commandment: "You shall not have other gods beside me" (Ex 20:3).

In sum, when Catholics receive the Eucharist—the true, real, and substantial presence of the body, blood, soul, and divinity of Jesus Christ—we receive fully the fruits of his sacrifice on the cross. This is possible, as we discussed at length in the previous chapter, because at the Last Supper Jesus commanded his followers: "Do this in memory of me." His words mean that the Eucharist makes his sacrifice on the cross present and accessible today and always.

Chapter Four

The Eucharist and Deification

*You will not change me into you like the food your
flesh eats, but you will be changed into me.*

The Voice from on High,
speaking to St. Augustine

Introduction

"The Mass is boring." This is a common complaint many Catholics make about the liturgy, especially those whose parents dragged them to Mass every week as children. Among other objections, some Catholics feel that the Mass is painfully repetitious because they hear the same prayers week after week. One prayer, however, is prayed by the priest during Mass that is unknown to many Catholics. Toward the beginning of the Liturgy of the Eucharist, the faithful bring forward the gifts of bread and wine to the altar. The priest then holds the paten with the bread slightly above the altar and says, "Blessed are you, Lord God of all creation, for through your goodness we have received the bread we offer you: fruit of the earth and work of human hands, it will become for us the bread of life." He then pours wine and a little water into the chalice and inaudibly whispers, "By the mystery of this water and wine may we come to share in the divinity of Christ who humbled himself to share in our humanity."

In a letter to a certain Caecilius, St. Cyprian of Carthage explains the spiritual significance of mingling the water and the wine: "We see that in the water is understood the people, but in the wine is shown the blood of Christ. But when the water is mingled in the chalice with the wine, the people are made one with Christ."[81] Cyprian's claim that we are "made one with Christ" in the mingling of Christ's divinity and our humanity is echoed in Augustine's *Confessions*. In Book Seven, Augustine, now a bishop reflecting back on his initial stirrings of knowledge about God, says that he heard God's "voice from on high" telling him, "'I am the food of the fully grown; grow and you will feed on me. And you will not change me into you like the food your flesh eats, but you will be changed into me.'"[82]

The Mass, Cyprian, and Augustine all point to the Church's teaching that, when we receive the Eucharist, a "progressive transfiguration,"[83] as Benedict XVI calls it, forms us into Christ by allowing us to participate in his divine life. This transformational process is often described by the technical term "deification." In this chapter, we will define and explore the concept of deification, investigate some of its biblical and patristic roots, describe how the Eucharist is the primary means of deification, discuss the fruits of deification, and offer two biblical examples of interior transformation caused by personal encounters with Jesus.

Deification

In the fourth century, St. Gregory of Nazianzus coined the Greek term "*theosis*" to describe this transformational process.[84] In contemporary English, that term is usually rendered as "deification," although sometimes "divinization" is also used. "Deification" comes from the Latin words *deus* and *facere*, which together mean "to make into God."[85] Although this basic etymological definition is a good place to start, other definitions help clarify what deification means. Late in the fifth century, Pseudo-Dionysius the Areopagite defined deification as "the attaining of likeness to God and union with him so far as possible."[86] Several recent scholars also have offered their own definitions.[87] Jared Ortiz has said that "deification is the process by which the Holy Spirit unites us to the Father by conforming us to Christ." Deification begins in this life with the first touch of God's grace—either in baptism or in the first stirrings of faith which lead to baptism—but is not completed until after the resurrection in the next life. Through the power of the Holy Spirit, especially in the sacraments, we are united to God and, while never ceasing to be human, our union with God transforms us into the one to whom we are united.[88]

Deification has become controversial in some non-Catholic and even Catholic circles because, for some, the claim that we can be united to God is idolatrous as it confuses God and humanity. Deification, however, never blurs the line between Creator and creature because those who are deified do not attain the likeness of God in nature, but only in grace. Augustine makes this clear: "It is evident, then, as he [Christ] has called men gods, that they are deified by his grace, not born of his substance. . . . If we have been made sons of God, we have also been made gods: but this is the effect of grace adopting, not nature generating."[89]

This adoption is rooted in participation in Christ. We have seen this theme of participation several times already in this book. In the previous two chapters, we saw that Catholics participate in the fruits of Christ's sacrificial offering through the memorial re-presentation of the cross. With deification, we once again return to this theme of participation. "If God is the source of all being," Daniel Keating has said, "then we as creatures participate in his being. We do not share or participate in the divine being as God himself possesses it. Rather, we share in his being in that he gives us our created being by bringing us into existence. He has it essentially;

we have it derivatively and by participation. He is being; we participate in being."[90]

Biblical and Patristic Roots of Deification

Many theological words or phrases in the Christian lexicon are taken directly from the Bible, such as "justification" (Rom 5:17), "sanctification" (Rom 6:22), and "righteousness" (Rom 9:30). Others trace their conceptual roots to the Bible, even if the exact words are not found in it, such as "Trinity" (Mt 28:19), "transubstantiation" (1 Cor 11:24), and "pope" (Mt 16:18). The word "deification" is not used by any biblical author, but the theological idea can be found in Christianity from the beginning. Four biblical passages that are foundational for the development of deification will be discussed here, two from the Old Testament and two from the New Testament.

The first relevant Old Testament passage comes from one of the two creation narratives in Genesis: "Then God said: Let us make human beings in our image, after our likeness. Let them have dominion over the fish of the sea, the birds of the air, the tame animals, all the wild animals, and the creatures that crawl on the earth. God created mankind in his image; in the image of God he created them; male and female he created them" (1:26-27). This inexhaustibly rich passage is important for different aspects of the Catholic intellectual tradition, including the moral and social traditions, because it points to the inviolable dignity of the human person.[91] For our purposes, it suggests that if God, who is a communion of three persons (Father, Son, and Holy Spirit), has created human beings in his image and likeness, it must be concluded that we are also created for communion. This means that the only communion that truly will cause our restless hearts to find rest is communion with the uncreated Creator. Communion with other created beings, including a spouse, a child, or a friend, only partially satisfies. Inscribed into our being is the need to share in the very life of the God who created us in his image and likeness.[92]

The second Old Testament passage pointing to deification comes from Psalm 82:

> A psalm of Asaph.
>
> God takes a stand in the divine council,
> gives judgment in the midst of the gods.
> "How long will you judge unjustly
> and favor the cause of the wicked?
>
> *Selah*
>
> "Defend the lowly and fatherless;
> render justice to the afflicted and needy.
> Rescue the lowly and poor;
> deliver them from the hand of the wicked."
> The gods neither know nor understand,
> wandering about in darkness,
> and all the world's foundations shake.
> I declare: "Gods though you be,
> offspring of the Most High all of you,
> Yet like any mortal you shall die;
> like any prince you shall fall."
> Arise, O God, judge the earth,
> for yours are all the nations.

In this psalm, the most important verses related to deification are verse 1 ("God takes a stand in divine council, gives judgment in the midst of the gods"), and verses 6 and 7 ("I declare: 'Gods though you may be, offspring of the Most High all of you, yet like any mortal you shall die; like any prince you shall fall'"). The rabbinic tradition interprets these verses as referring both to Adam and Eve, as well as the Israelites wandering in the desert. Even though Adam and Eve were "gods" (that is, immortal and impassible), and had been commanded not to eat from the tree of the knowledge of good and evil, they had rebelled. The Israelites, likewise, transgressed the Ten Commandments they received from Moses by falling into the sin of idolatry when they worshiped the golden calf. Adam, Eve, and the Israelites justly received the punishment that "like any mortal you shall die; like any prince you shall fall."

St. Justin Martyr follows this Jewish interpretation,[93] but, because of the advent of Christ, the adopted "offspring of the Most High" may avoid death.[94] Adam, Eve, and the Israelites, as Norman Russell has said, "failed to become gods and children of God through their disobedience; but Christians have succeeded in becoming precisely that through their obedience to Christ. Conforming to Christ has restored them to Adam's divine state."[95] When Christians participate in the divine life of Christ, the effects of the transgressions of our ancestors are reversed.

The first New Testament passage that is relevant for deification comes from Paul's Second Letter to the Corinthians: "For you know the gracious act of our Lord Jesus Christ, that for your sake he became poor although he was rich, so that by his poverty you might become rich" (8:9). The poverty and riches of Jesus that Paul describes are spiritual. Jesus did not come to make his adopted sons and daughters financially wealthy. Christ's riches are his divinity, while his poverty is understood as our humanity. This is often described as the "exchange formula" because, in becoming human, Christ exchanged his riches (divinity) for our poverty (humanity); and in participating in Christ, we exchange our poverty (humanity) for his riches (divinity).[96] Joseph Ratzinger, Pope Benedict XVI, explains that "this exchange consists of God taking upon himself our human existence in order to bestow his divine existence upon us, of his choosing our nothingness in order to give us his plenitude."[97] Although Ratzinger, like Paul, does not explicitly use the word deification here, his explanation of Jesus' "divine existence" and "plenitude" given to humanity speaks to the heart of this teaching.

The second New Testament passage relevant for our conversation comes from The Second Letter of Peter: "His [Jesus'] divine power has bestowed on us everything that makes for life and devotion, through the knowledge of him who called us by his own glory and power. Through these, he has bestowed on us the precious and very great promises, so that through them you may come to share in the divine nature, after escaping from the corruption that is in the world because of evil desire" (1:3-4).[98] This sharing or participating in the divine nature is the *telos*, or end, of the Christian life. In fact, the very first paragraph of the *Catechism of the Catholic Church* points to divine participation as the reason why God created humankind: "God, infinitely perfect and blessed in himself, in a plan of sheer goodness freely created man to make him share in his own blessed life."[99]

Over the centuries, theologians have developed the concept of deification that can be discerned in these and other biblical passages. For the sake of brevity, we will restrict ourselves in this section to exploring two Church Fathers, the Greek-speaking Athanasius of Alexandria, and the Latin-speaking Augustine, to show how the Tradition expanded the biblical idea of deification.

Athanasius, one of the most important Doctors of the Church, became the great defender of the Council of Nicaea (325 AD), which defined the relationship between the Father and the Son as "consubstantial," that is, having the "same essence." In doing so, Nicaea rejected and anathematized the presbyter Arius of Alexandria, who claimed that the Father and the Son are not the same essence. In his text *On the Incarnation*, Athanasius describes why the Word, the second person of the Trinity, became man. Through his incarnation, the Word "has been declared; through his bodiliness, we can see the mind of the invisible Father; through his death, we do

not die; through his inability to suffer, he healed our suffering."
He then claims that "he [Jesus], indeed, assumed humanity
that we might become God."[100] This phrase by Athanasius
distills the "exchange formula" into its most cogent expression.

As with Athanasius in the East, deification is also found in
the writings of Augustine in the West. Earlier in this chapter,
we saw how Genesis 1:26 ("Let us make human beings in our
image, after our likeness") is one of the foundational biblical
texts for deification. This was the sixth day of creation (Gn
1:24-31). At the end of each of the first five days, we are told that
God proclaimed the goodness of his various creations. At the
end of the sixth day, however, God did not declare the goodness
of human beings. Rather, God "looked at everything he had
made, and found it very good" (Gn 1:31). In other words, God
did not explicitly point to the goodness of humanity as he did to
his creations at the end of the other five days; on the sixth day,
he declared "everything" good. Augustine interprets this as an
indication of humanity's incompleteness. This incompleteness
was deliberate on God's part. According to Augustine, at some
point in the future God intended to make humans more than
human, but sin prevented this. This incompleteness, moreover,
is manifest in Adam and Eve's capitulation to the snake's
enticement to eat the fruit from the tree of the knowledge of
good and evil. If Adam and Eve lacked nothing, they would
not have desired to become "like gods" (Gn 3:5).[101]

Created in God's image and likeness, Adam's unfinished
nature cried out to be completed—a completion that is accomplished only by participation in what Augustine labeled
the "whole Christ" (totus Christus). The whole Christ is a
development on the Pauline idea of the Church as the body
of Christ. In his First Letter to the Corinthians, Paul insists,
"Now you are Christ's body, and individually parts of it. Some
people God has designated in the Church to be, first, apostles;
second, prophets; third, teachers; then, mighty deeds; then,
gifts of healing, assistance, administration, and varieties of

tongues" (12:27-28). Through the centuries, this passage has been understood to mean that, through baptism, Christians have become incorporated into Christ's mystical body. But Augustine takes Paul a step further. By becoming united with Christ in his mystical body, Christians don't simply become connected or united to Jesus; Christians become transformed into Christ: "Let us congratulate ourselves then and give thanks for having been made not only Christians but Christ. Do you understand, brothers and sisters, the grace of God upon us; do you grasp that? Be filled with wonder, rejoice and be glad: we have been made Christ. For, if he is the head, and we the members, then he and we are the whole man."[102]

The Eucharist and Deification

Deification begins, like all things, with God's gracious activity. Usually, it commences at baptism, but it can happen any time that God moves us toward him.[103] After baptism, the sacraments of Confirmation, Reconciliation, Anointing of the Sick, Holy Orders, and Matrimony all strengthen and deepen this spiritual growth. But the sacrament of the Eucharist is the primary means of becoming more fully unified and conformed to Christ.[104] Receiving the Eucharist daily or weekly mysteriously infuses Christ's body, blood, soul, and divinity into us. "By partaking of the body and blood of Christ," St. Cyril of Jerusalem preached to catechumens in the fourth century, "may you be made of the same body and the same blood with him. For this is how we come to bear Christ in us, because his body and blood are distributed through our members; thus it is that, according to the blessed Peter, 'we become partakers of the divine nature' (2 Pt 1:4)."[105] In receiving the Eucharist "through our members," we abide ever more deeply in Christ because we do not receive him into our bodies alone (Jn 15:4); we receive him into our entire being.[106]

Early Christian authors are not alone in insisting that the Eucharist allows us to share in the divine nature. In our own age, Chiara Lubich, the founder of the Focolare Movement, echoes the fourth-century saint of Jerusalem: "This is the purpose of the Eucharist: to make us God (by participation). By mixing our flesh with Christ's life-giving flesh, which is given life by the Holy Spirit, the Eucharist divinizes us in soul and body. Therefore it makes us God."[107] This "mixing," as Thomas Merton writes, transforms us: "This sacrament is not given to us merely in order that we do something, but that we may *be* someone: that we may be Christ."[108]

The Fruits of Deification

Although the fruits of deification from the Eucharist are numerous, we will focus on three of the most important: forgiveness of sins, moral transformation, and an increase in holiness.

The Eucharistic Prayers during Mass and the Gospel of Matthew both assert that the primary fruit of sharing in the divine life of Christ through the Eucharist is "the forgiveness of sins" (Mt 26:28).[109] The sins wiped away in the Eucharist are technically called "venial."[110] According to the *Catechism of the Catholic Church*, "One commits venial sin when, in a less serious matter, he does not observe the standard prescribed by the moral law, or when he disobeys the moral law in a grave matter, but without full knowledge or without complete consent."[111] In plainer language, a venial sin has a minor degree of seriousness; or if it has greater seriousness, it is committed without full knowledge of its sinfulness, or without the complete consent of the will. The Eucharist, however, "is not ordered to the forgiveness of mortal sins."[112] Mortal sin consists in "a grave matter . . . also committed with full knowledge and deliberate consent."[113] These are properly forgiven in the Sacrament of Reconciliation.[114] Catholics who have not confessed mortal sins must refrain from receiving the Eucharist.[115] In addition to cleansing the previous venial sins of those who receive it, the Eucharist also helps them persevere in avoiding future sins,[116] both venial and mortal.[117]

Receiving the Eucharist, as Benedict XVI has stated, brings about a "moral urgency born of welcoming Jesus into our lives,"[118] which is the second important fruit of the Eucharist. Specifically, the Eucharist nourishes and provides growth in the moral virtues.[119] A virtue, according to the Greek philosopher Aristotle and echoed by the Catholic moral tradition, is a good habit. In the moral life, a habit is understood not in a negative sense—like mindlessly biting your fingernails, but in a positive sense—like regularly eating healthily. The four most fundamental virtues are called "cardinal," coming from the Latin word *cardo*, which means "hinge." Like the small but necessary hinge on a door, the cardinal virtues allow our moral lives to operate smoothly. The four cardinal virtues are justice (the good habit of giving to others what is due), temperance (the good habit of having rightly-ordered desires), fortitude (the good habit of courage), and prudence (the good habit of seeing the world as it actually is, and making a plan accordingly).[120] These four virtues and their associated habits are universal; they can be fostered regardless of religion, politics, or philosophy. Three other virtues, called "theological virtues," however, are unique to the Christian tradition. These are faith (the good habit that allows us to believe in the truths about our relationship to God, and God's relationship to us), hope (the good habit oriented toward the life of the world to come), and charity (the good habit that allows us to love God for God's sake, and to love everything else in God). They are called theological because they are directly related to God in a way that the cardinal virtues are not (1 Cor 13:13; 1 Thes 1:3).[121]

This moral transformation leads to a third fruit of the Eucharist: an increase in holiness. Throughout the Bible, God is described as holy. In the Old Testament, God tells Moses,

"Speak to the whole Israelite community and tell them: Be holy, for I, the Lord your God, am holy" (Lv 19:2).[122] In the Book of Isaiah, one seraphim cries out to another, "Holy, holy, holy is the Lord of hosts! All the earth is filled with his glory!" (Is 6:3). The Hebrew word usually translated as "holy" is *kadosh*, which literally means "set apart," or "separate." God, in other words, is set apart or separate from other gods (Ex 20:3), and from creation. When God calls the Israelites to be holy as he is holy, he is telling them that they must be set apart from other nations. For us today, this means (among other things) that God calls us to be set apart from the secular world (Rom 12:2).

The English word "saint" comes from the Latin word *sanctus*, which means "holy." The saints of our tradition, the "cloud of witnesses" (Heb 12:1), are the holy men and women who have set themselves apart from the world for God. Usually when we think of saints, we think of those who have reached the highest levels of devotion to God, like St. John Henry Newman, St. Teresa of Calcutta, or St. John Paul II. Vatican II, however, emphasized that all people, not just the spiritual elites, are called to be saints. For the saints, and for all of us as we answer the "universal call to holiness,"[123] such sanctification is achieved "with maximum effectiveness"[124] through our encounter with Jesus in the Eucharist.[125]

Biblical Examples

Throughout the Bible and the history of the Church, there are countless examples of individuals being transformed by Christ, but we will limit ourselves to two. The first is the story of Zacchaeus the tax collector, which is found only in the Gospel of Luke:

> [Jesus] came to Jericho and intended to pass through the town. Now a man there named Zacchaeus, who

was a chief tax collector and also a wealthy man, was seeking to see who Jesus was; but he could not see him because of the crowd, for he was short in stature. So he ran ahead and climbed a sycamore tree in order to see Jesus, who was about to pass that way. When he reached the place, Jesus looked up and said to him, "Zacchaeus, come down quickly, for today I must stay at your house." And he came down quickly and received him with joy. When they all saw this, they began to grumble, saying, "He has gone to stay at the house of a sinner." But Zacchaeus stood there and said to the Lord, "Behold, half of my possessions, Lord, I shall give to the poor, and if I have extorted anything from anyone I shall repay it four times over." And Jesus said to him, "Today salvation has come to this house because this man too is a descendant of Abraham. For the Son of Man has come to seek and to save what was lost." (19:1-10)

Jewish society reviled tax collectors such as Matthew (Mt 9:7-11), Levi (Mk 2:14), and Zacchaeus for two reasons. First, they were considered thieves, because they collected more money than they needed and kept the surplus for themselves. Because he was "a wealthy man," the author hints that Zacchaeus stole a significant amount. Second, tax collectors were considered traitors because they exacted money from their fellow Jews on behalf of the oppressive Roman Gentiles.

Zacchaeus is presented as financially wealthy, but morally bankrupt. As the story continues, this bankruptcy is reinforced by being "short in stature." St. Cyril of Alexandria interprets his physical size to mean that he was spiritually small. Zacchaeus looks for Jesus, Cyril writes, "but the multitude prevented him, not so much that of the people, as of his sins; and he was little of stature, not merely in a bodily point of view, but also spiritually."[126] Fortunately, his spiritual stature does not prevent him from persisting; he climbs a sycamore tree in order to see Jesus. We all need to climb the tree, according to Cyril, to overcome our passionate attachments: "In no other way can a man see Christ and believe in Him, except by mounting up into the sycamore, by rendering foolish his [bodily] members which are upon the earth, fornication, uncleanness, etc."[127]

When Jesus sees Zacchaeus, he tells him to come down because "today I must stay at your house." Zacchaeus' "house" is spiritually significant because it represents his interior life. This same spiritual representation takes place during the liturgy. Before receiving the Eucharist, Catholics pray "Lord, I am not worthy that you should enter under my roof, but only say the word and my soul shall be healed," an allusion to the centurion who, when asking Jesus to heal his servant, said "Lord, I am not worthy to have you enter under my roof; only say the word and my servant will be healed" (Mt 8:8). To receive Jesus into our "house" or under our "roof" is to receive him into our heart. When Jesus is received into the tax collector's house "with joy," the crowd bitterly accuses Zacchaeus of being a sinner. In the Bible, no one is exempt from sin: "All have sinned and are deprived of the glory of God" (Rom 3:23). But those singled out as sinners are those who persist and revel in the sin. Zacchaeus must have boasted of his wealth throughout Jericho. His encounter with Jesus changes him; he gives half of his wealth to the poor and repays fourfold anyone from whom he had extorted. This radical change of heart and actions brought about the greatest fruit that encountering Jesus produces: "Today salvation has come to this house" (19:9).

The second story, also from the Gospel of Luke, provides an obvious example of interior transformation caused by encountering Christ in the Eucharist:

> Now that very day two of them were going to a village seven miles from Jerusalem called Emmaus, and they were conversing about all the things that had

occurred. And it happened that while they were
conversing and debating, Jesus himself drew near
and walked with them, but their eyes were prevented
from recognizing him. He asked them, "What are
you discussing as you walk along?" They stopped,
looking downcast. One of them, named Cleopas,
said to him in reply, "Are you the only visitor to
Jerusalem who does not know of the things that have
taken place there in these days?" And he replied to
them, "What sort of things?" They said to him, "The
things that happened to Jesus the Nazarene, who was
a prophet mighty in deed and word before God and
all the people, how our chief priests and rulers both
handed him over to a sentence of death and crucified
him. But we were hoping that he would be the one to
redeem Israel; and besides all this, it is now the third
day since this took place. Some women from our
group, however, have astounded us: they were at the
tomb early in the morning and did not find his body;
they came back and reported that they had indeed
seen a vision of angels who announced that he was
alive. Then some of those with us went to the tomb
and found things just as the women had described,
but him they did not see." And he said to them, "Oh,
how foolish you are! How slow of heart to believe all
that the prophets spoke! Was it not necessary that
the Messiah should suffer these things and enter into
his glory?" Then beginning with Moses and all the
prophets, he interpreted to them what referred to him
in all the scriptures. As they approached the village
to which they were going, he gave the impression
that he was going on farther. But they urged him,
"Stay with us, for it is nearly evening and the day is
almost over." So he went in to stay with them. And
it happened that, while he was with them at table,

he took bread, said the blessing, broke it, and gave
it to them. With that their eyes were opened and
they recognized him, but he vanished from their
sight. Then they said to each other, "Were not our
hearts burning [within us] while he spoke to us on
the way and opened the scriptures to us?" So they
set out at once and returned to Jerusalem where they
found gathered together the eleven and those with
them who were saying, "The Lord has truly been
raised and has appeared to Simon!" Then the two
recounted what had taken place on the way and how
he was made known to them in the breaking of the
bread. (24:13-35)

At the beginning of the story, two of Jesus' followers are walking
away from Jerusalem toward a village called Emmaus because
the crucifixion convinced them that Jesus would not "be the one
to redeem Israel." On a physical level, this verse tells us that they
are going from point A to point B. On a spiritual level, it points
to something deeper—their spiritual location.[128] As Augustine
puts it: "They had wandered off the way."[129] When Jesus drew
near and began to walk with them, they "were walking along,
dead, with Christ alive. They were walking along, dead, with
life itself. Life was walking along with them, but in their hearts
life had not yet been restored."[130] They do not recognize Jesus;
"Their eyes were prevented from recognizing him" because
their lack of faith blinded them spiritually.

When Jesus inquires about their conversation, they ask
"Are you the only visitor to Jerusalem who does not know of
the things that have taken place there in these days?" The im-
patience and bite in Cleopas' tone is evident. His nastiness is
a symptom of his disordered heart. When we walk away from
Jerusalem—the place of Jesus' resurrection—our spiritual lives
unravel.[131] The disciples then tell him about the crucifixion
and the empty tomb. Jesus calls them "foolish" and explains

how Moses, the prophets, and all the Scriptures predicted the Messiah, but they still do not recognize their companion's identity.[132] As they approach the village at sunset, the two disciples invite Jesus to stay with them. While at table, Jesus "Took bread, said the blessing, broke it, and gave it to them," an obvious reference to the Eucharist.[133] Then, and only then, are their eyes opened, and they recognize him. They then realize that their hearts had been burning while Jesus, who they could not recognize, was speaking. Then they set out "at once" back to Jerusalem.[134] The story reaches its climax with the two disciples telling the others how Jesus "was made known to them" in the breaking of the bread. In other words, the interiority of the two disciples was transformed by the blessed and broken bread. Spiritually, the Eucharist placed them back on the way toward Jerusalem.

Chapter Five

The Eucharist and Unity

Because the loaf of bread is one, we, though many, are
one body, for we all partake of the one loaf.

St. Paul

Introduction

Before he and his disciples went out across the Kidron Valley
to the garden where he was arrested, Jesus prayed for his disciples: "Holy Father, keep them in your name that you have
given me, so that they may be one just as we are" (Jn 17:11).
Then, Jesus petitioned the Father for those "who will believe
in me through their [the disciples'] word." (17:20). He prayed
that "they may all be one, as you, Father, are in me and I in you,
that they also may be in us, that. . . the world may believe that
you sent me . . . . that they may be one, as we are one, I in them
and you in me, that they may be brought to perfection as one"
(17:20-22). Unity is clearly one of Jesus' highest concerns—if
not *the* highest concern—for humanity and is accomplished
primarily through the Eucharist.[135]

   This chapter will explore unity as a fruit of the Eucharist. As Joseph Ratzinger summarized it, "The purpose of
the Eucharist is the transformation of those who receive it
in authentic communion. And so the end is unity, that peace
which we—separate individuals who live beside one another
or in conflict with one another—. . . . become with Christ and
in him, as one organism of self-giving, to live in view of the

Resurrection and the new world."[136] Ratzinger's point will become clearer through a biblical example of how sin has caused disunity in the Church. Second, we will investigate how opening ourselves up to intimacy through conversation over a meal and wine creates social bonds of friendship, or kinship. We will discuss how the Eucharist reverses the disunity in the human family caused by sin. Then, we will survey different signs that manifest the unity of the Church. Finally, we will describe how the Eucharist was a unifying response to the atomizing effects of torture of the Pinochet regime in Chile.

Disunity Caused by Sin

The community Paul found in Corinth demonstrates how, from the beginning, sin has caused division in the Church. Many were jealous, rivalrous (1 Cor 3:3), and inflated with pride (4:18). One was living in an incestuous relationship with the wife of his father (5:1), and the community was proud of it (5:2). Some were immoral and greedy; there were idolaters, slanderers, drunkards, and thieves (5:11); some solicited prostitutes (6:15-20), disregarded weaker brothers, and offered sacrifices in pagan temples.

The division was manifested in a variety of ways. Among other complaints, Paul said that the community had lost its unified mind and purpose (1:10). He had heard from "Chloe's people" that factions had arisen (1:11). Some claimed to belong to Paul, while others to Apollos, to Cephas, or to Christ (1:12). Some had brought their disputes to be adjudicated in the pagan Roman courts, rather than to the "holy ones" (6:1-10). Paul hinted that unnamed individuals were passing judgment on him, denying his right to act like the other apostles and questioning his right to work (9:1-27). Some were divided over the teaching on Christ's resurrection, and on the resurrection of the body (15:1-58).

The Corinthians' most serious manifestation of division, however, concerned the *agape* meal. When gathered for the breaking of the bread, each person would eat his own meal. Some did not have enough to eat, while others got drunk. Paul warned that, before eating the blessed bread and drinking from the chalice, they must examine themselves. Those who ate and drank unworthily would eat and drink judgment on themselves. "This is why," Paul said, "many among you are ill and infirm, and a considerable number are dying. If we discerned ourselves, we would not be under judgment; but since we are judged by the Lord, we are being disciplined so that we may not be condemned along with the world" (1 Cor 11:30-32). Paul then ordered that, when they gathered together, they must wait for each other, and eat their personal meals at home (11:17-34).

A Meal and Unity

Why is eating at a restaurant the classic first-date activity? Eating in front of someone that you don't know well and are trying to impress is dangerous. Countless mistakes could leave you embarrassed. You could get spaghetti on your shirt. You could have broccoli in your teeth and not know it. You could knock over your glass, spilling your wine. Despite countless social landmines, people are willing to traverse this field in hopes of forming a relationship. Why do people fly across the country every November just to eat with people they may not like very much? The cost of the flight, hotel, car rental, gas, time, and effort seem ludicrous. And yet families go to great lengths for this secular ritual.

The short answer is that sharing a meal (not just eating food) has an ineffable power to create social ties among strangers, acquaintances, friends, families, and even enemies. In *The Hungry Soul: Eating and the Perfecting of our Nature*,

Leon Kass offers some insights about how sharing a meal and wine creates these bonds of unity. He points out that eating at table—as opposed to eating on the run or facing the television—reorders us into a different social space. It removes us from the cares and concerns of life and commits us to a plan that includes the thoughtful preparation of the meal guided by a menu. It also commits us to a "form and formality" which specifies a code of conduct that includes facing each other, and "commensurate forms of commensal behavior." This "commensal behavior" includes, among other things, a hospitality of generosity.[137]

Often, a key element of a shared meal is wine, "which gladdens the heart" (Ps 104:15). Ecclesiasticus claims that "wine is very life to anyone, if taken in moderation. Does anyone really live who lacks the wine which from the beginning was created for joy? Joy of heart, good cheer, and delight is wine enough, drunk at the proper time" (Sir 31:27-28). Wine is the social lubricant that facilitates trust and intimacy among those around the table. When imbibed temperately, it allows us to let down our walls, to unwind, and to loosen our tongues.[138]

Sharing a meal, as Kass puts it, is little more than "an 'excuse' for conversation."[139] While food and drink revivify the body, conversation revivifies the soul. It allows us to open ourselves up to vulnerability, and to share our innermost thoughts, hopes, feelings, fears, and aspirations. At Thanksgiving, we catch a glimpse, over a second helping of stuffing, or a third glass of Chianti, of the essence of our aunt as she shares her personal struggles. In turn, over the sweetness of a generous piece of pumpkin pie, we share our own struggles. We can talk on the telephone, over Skype, on a park bench, or on a bus. But there is something real—yet indefinable—about how breaking bread and sharing wine are catalysts for intimacy that cannot be found in any other way.[140] Though it cannot be explained exactly, we all have experienced it. This mutuality is the stuff that makes life worth living.

Conversation over a meal can create new friendships and deepen old ones. Plutarch, the Platonist philosopher, understood the "friend-making character of the table." He said that "a guest comes to share not only meat, wine, and dessert, but conversation, fun, and the amiability that leads to friendship."[141] Today's culture often reduces friends to little more than "wing men" on a Friday night helping each other achieve their latest sexual conquests, or "drinking buddies" watching sporting events together. Christian friendship is not based on the desire for personal gain.[142] "Only the ties of a friendship," wrote the monk John Cassian, "which is founded upon similarity of virtuousness are trustworthy and indissoluble."[143] In other words, a true friendship is grounded not in profit, use, or pleasure, but in the desire for the good and virtue of the other. Such selfless desire can be expressed and deepened during a festive repast.

Breaking bread together also can establish kinship. In *Tattoos on the Heart: The Power of Boundless Compassion*, Fr. Greg Boyle defines it as "not serving the other, but being one with the other."[144] Echoing St. Teresa of Calcutta, Boyle says that we have forgotten that we belong to each other. "Kinship," he says, "is what happens to us when we refuse to let that happen. With kinship as the objective, other essential things fall into place; without it, no justice, no peace. I suspect that were kinship our goal, we would no longer be promoting justice—we would be celebrating it."[145] Boyle demonstrates such kinship in his work with Homeboy Industries, his gang rehabilitation program. He jokes, laughs, and cries with the gang members and former gang members he does not serve, but with whom he lives. Many of his stories of kinship happen over a meal.

Boyle recounts how a meal shared among prisoners created unexpected bonds of kinship. He had been ministering to inmates on an island off the coast of Mexico. In the morning, he would make bricks with the prisoners, in the afternoon celebrate Mass with them, and in the evening play games.

One morning, Beto, one of the prisoners, told Boyle to meet him at noon at the garden of one of the lieutenants. When Boyle arrived, Beto jumped over the garden fence and started stuffing his shirt with vegetables. Neither had eaten vegetables—or anything palatable—in recent memory. They fled to a remote area of the prison where Beto boiled the vegetables with an iguana that he had hidden in a cloth sack. Capturing iguanas was prohibited, and both could have been beaten, not to mention the punishment for stealing the vegetables. The scent from the boiling pot began attracting other prisoners. First, an older prisoner arrived. Beto invited him to join them and added some water to the pot. Rather than sitting down, the man went back to his cell to retrieve some salt he had been saving. Then, another prisoner arrived. Beto added more water and vegetables to the pot. This prisoner went back to his cell to retrieve a jalapeno he had been saving and added it to the mix. Yet another prisoner arrived and, after he was invited to stay, went to his cell to fetch a can of tomato paste he had been hiding. By the time the stew was finished, about eight people were sitting around the cauldron expectantly. "Plenty to go around," Boyle said, "and just as tasty as it could be. Everyone brought his flavor to this forbidden pot of iguana stew, and keeping anyone away and excluded was unthinkable to this band of prisoners. Alone, they didn't have much, but together, they had a potful of plenty."[146]

It is hard to imagine someone inviting strangers, mere acquaintances, or even enemies to sit at table like that. It is even harder to imagine men living in an institution designed to foster disunity and isolation sharing their precious bounty. But Beto demonstrates that, even in a divisive place, the small gesture of love through a meal can establish kinship.

Jesus, like Beto, often reclined at table and ate with undesirables, like sinners and tax collectors.[147] This inflamed the Pharisees' ire because they sensed that Jesus was creating bonds of unity with those who shared at his table—a unity with the "other" that was intolerable, especially to a group whose name comes from a Hebrew word that means the "separated ones."

Like our previous story of Jesus eating with Zacchaeus, another story also demonstrates Jesus' table fellowship. Jesus saw Levi, a tax collector, sitting at the customs post. Without any introduction or explanation, he invited Levi to follow him, which he did. At a banquet that Levi hosted, a great number of tax collectors reclined with him and with Jesus. The Pharisees and scribes complained, asking "'Why do you eat and drink with tax collectors and sinners?' Jesus said to them in reply, 'Those who are heathy do not need a physician, but the sick do. I have not come to call the righteousness to repentance but sinners'" (Lk 5:27-32; Mk 2:14-17). Unlike a medical doctor, Jesus responded not to sinners' physical needs but to their spiritual diseases by counteracting their social alienation through the integrating force of commensality.

The Eucharist and Unity

The human division caused by sin is healed first by being united to Christ, then, through Christ, to each other.[148] Unity begins with baptism. As Paul said, "for in one Spirit we were all baptized into one body" (1 Cor 12:13). In this "one body," Paul also said, "there is neither Jew nor Greek, there is neither slave nor free person, there is not male and female; for you are all one in Christ Jesus" (Gal 3:28). The divisions that the fallen world emphasizes—race, socioeconomic status, and gender— dissolve in the regenerating waters of baptism.

After baptism, unity is strengthened and deepened by the Eucharist.[149] Paul articulates this in his warning about the dangers of eating meat sacrificed to pagan idols. He asked the community in Corinth, "The cup of blessing that we bless, is it not a participation in the blood of Christ? The bread that we break, is it not a participation in the body of Christ?" (1

Cor 10:16). His audience did not grasp that eating sacrificed meat made them participate in demons. They needed to stop doing so because they already were participating in Christ by eating and drinking his body and blood. Paul explained, "Because the loaf of bread is one, we, though many, are one body, for we all partake of the one loaf" (1 Cor 10:17). When we, disintegrated sinners, receive and share in the one loaf, we become one body because, through the Eucharist, we receive and participate in the one person of Christ.[150]

Although the Church manifests herself in different cultures and in different locations throughout time, the Church is fundamentally one because she is constituted by the Eucharist. We announce this unity each week during Mass when we proclaim that we believe in "*one*, holy, Catholic, and apostolic Church."[151] This unity is not a collection of individuals loosely connected like computers on a decentralized internet web. As Paul says to the community in Corinth, it is a unity of different parts of a body coming together:

> Now the body is not a single part, but many. . . . God placed the parts, each one of them, in the body as he intended. If they were all one part, where would the body be? But as it is, there are many parts, yet one body. . . . God has so constructed the body as to give greater honor to a part that is without it, so that there may be no division in the body, but that the parts may have the same concern for one another. If [one] part suffers, all the parts suffer with it; if one part is honored, all the parts share its joy. (1 Cor 12:14-26)

In *On the Unity of the Church*, St. Cyprian poetically describes how to imagine the multiplicity but ultimate unity of the Church:

> The Church also is one, which is spread abroad far and wide into a multitude by an increase of fruitfulness. As there are many rays of the sun, but one light;

and many branches of a tree, but one strength based
in its tenacious root; and since from one spring flow
many streams, although the multiplicity seems dif-
fused in the liberality of an overflowing abundance,
yet the unity is still preserved in the source. Separate
a ray of the sun from its body of light, its unity does
not allow a division of light; break a branch from a
tree—when broken, it will not be able to bud; cut off
the stream from its fountain, and that which is cut
off dries up.[152]

This unity, Cyprian continues, "comes from the divine strength
and coheres in celestial sacraments."[153]

The Church is one because the Church and Christ are one.
The encounter between Saul of Tarsus and Jesus demonstrates
that the relationship between Christ and those who "remain in
my love" (Jn 15:9) is not mere intimacy, but true unity. Saul, a
Pharisee, was a "zealot for my ancestral traditions" (Gal 1:14).
He viewed the "church of God" (Gal 1:13) as a corrupting
influence on Judaism. Saul and many other Jews feared that
the followers of Jesus would "change the customs that Moses
handed down to us" (Acts 6:14). This fear led Saul to consent
to the execution of the first martyr, Stephen (Acts 8:1), and to
enter house after house dragging out men and women alike
and handing them over to the authorities (Acts 8:3). He then
went to the high priest in Jerusalem to ask for letters to the
synagogue in Damascus giving him permission to bring back
in chains anyone "who belonged to the Way" (Acts 9:1-2). On
his journey to Damascus, a light from the sky flashed around
him, dashing him to the ground. He heard a voice say "'Saul,
Saul, why are you persecuting me?' He said, 'Who are you,
sir?' The reply came, 'I am Jesus, whom you are persecuting.
Now get up and go into the city and you will be told what you
must do'" (Acts 9:4). Note that Jesus did not ask Saul "Why
are you persecuting *my followers*?" He asked, "Why are you
persecuting *me*?" Jesus' question points to the unity between

Jesus and his followers. By persecuting Jesus' followers, Saul
was persecuting Jesus. Jesus and his followers are one. Saul
went to Damascus and after he regained his sight was baptized
immediately and changed his name to Paul. He proceeded to
become the most important evangelist in the history of the
Church (Acts 9:18).

The Eucharist does more than constitute the Church quantitatively. It also makes the body grow qualitatively because
it conforms the Church more closely to the image of Christ
himself.[154] In his encyclical *Ecclesia de Eucharistia*—usually
called *On the Eucharist*, but a translation closer to the Latin
would be *The Church Comes from the Eucharist*—John Paul II
claims the Church is "built up"[155] by the Eucharist, which also
"confirms" and "reinforces"[156] the Church. The *Catechism* puts
it another way: "Those who receive the Eucharist are united
more closely to Christ. Through it, Christ unites them to all
the faithful in one body—the Church. Communion renews,
strengthens, and deepens this incorporation into the Church,
already achieved by Baptism."[157]

Signs of Unity

The unity that Jesus wants is deeper than mere feelings of affection for others. Conversely, he does not desire a tyrannical
unity as demanded by the totalitarian regimes of the twentieth
century that executed anyone demonstrating individuality.
The New Testament and the Early Church offer multiple signs
signifying the true unity that Christ seeks. This section will
explore five of those signs.

The first sign can be seen in Paul's letter to the Galatians in
which he criticizes that community for having abandoned the
gospel message that he had preached to them. "I am amazed,"
he scolds them, "that you are so quickly forsaking the one who
called you by [the] grace [of Christ] for a different gospel (not

that there is another). But there are some who are disturbing you and wish to prevent the gospel of Christ" (Gal 1:6-7). For Paul, the oneness of the Deposit of Faith is foundational for the integrity of the Church. One community cannot believe a different faith than other communities, for the content of the faith is not of human origin—coming from Paul or any other preacher—but was revealed by Jesus (Gal 1:11-12).

In Ephesians, we see a second sign of unity. Prior to the Incarnation, Gentiles were "alienated from the community of Israel and strangers to the covenants of promise, without hope and without God in the world" (2:12-13). But because of Jesus, Gentiles now are "no longer strangers and sojourners" (2:19). Rather, they "have come near by the blood of Christ" (2:13), are "fellow citizens with the holy ones and members of the household of God," (2:19), and are "coheirs, members of the same body, and copartners in the promise of Christ Jesus through the gospel" (3:6). This reconciliation between Jews and Gentiles calls for a new "unity of the spirit through the bond of peace" (4:3) grounded in, and demonstrated by, the unity of "one body and one Spirit, as you were also called to the one hope of your call; one Lord, one faith, one baptism; one God and Father of all, who is over all and through all and in all" (4:4-6).

A third sign of unity is the financial assistance from wealthier communities to poorer communities.[158] More than a demonstration of generous hearts, it signifies an understanding of the connectedness of those within each community, and the connectedness of the different local communities to each other. In Galatians, for example, Paul writes that a revelation led him to Jerusalem[159] where he shared his preaching with the leadership. Some "false brothers" had criticized him because he did not require Gentile followers of Jesus to be circumcised (2:4). After listening to him, the leaders of the community discerned that Gentile followers of Jesus should not be forced to follow the Jewish Law. Rather, they recognized that the circumcised had been entrusted to Peter, and the uncircumcised to Paul. Paul then reports that James, Cephas, and John "gave me and Barnabas their right hands in partnership," and "that we were to be mindful of the poor, which is the very thing I was eager to do" (2:9-10). When preaching among the rich Gentile communities throughout the Mediterranean, Paul was asked to send money from them to the poorer community in Jerusalem.

In addition to financial assistance, Acts describes how Jesus' earliest followers shared possessions and lived communally, a fourth sign of unity. After Jesus' ascension into heaven, Peter gave a speech criticizing the Israelites in Jerusalem for crucifying Jesus (2:22-25). God, however, raised Jesus from the dead, and the Spirit was poured out at Pentecost (2:33), causing those who received "tongues as of fire" to speak in different languages (2:3-4). Those who heard Peter's speech were "cut to the heart," and asked what they should do. Peter told them to repent, be baptized, and to "save yourselves from this corrupt generation" (2:38-40). That day, about three thousand people were baptized. Acts then says that they "devoted themselves to the teaching of the apostles and to the communal life, to the breaking of the bread and to the prayers. . . . All who believed were together and had all things in common; they would sell their property and possessions and divide them among all according to each one's need" (2:42-44). Biblical scholar Daniel Harrington points out that the community in Jerusalem was not monastic, nor did it practice a form of proto-communism; they did not immediately sell everything they owned for the common good. Rather, those who owned property sold it as needs arose within the community, handing over the proceeds to be distributed (4:36-37; 5:1-11).[160]

In the second century, the Christian communities maintained those four marks of unity—unity of faith, unity between Jews and Gentiles, unity between rich and poor, and unity of the common life. By the second century, St. Ignatius of Antioch insisted that to be united to the Church also is to be united in communion with the local bishop, a fifth sign of unity. For Ignatius, the bishop is the representative of God on earth. Everything in the community, therefore, must be done with the consent of the bishop, including any actions by the presbyters and deacons.[161] "You should act in accord with the bishop's mind," he wrote to the community in Ephesus, "as you surely do. Your presbytery, indeed, which deserves its name and is a credit to God, is as closely tied to the bishop as the strings to a harp."[162] Those who did not act in accord "with the bishop's mind," or committed serious sins were excluded from Communion (because Communion was the visible expression of the bond of the unity of a local community with each other through their bishop) until they asked for forgiveness and were reconciled to the bishop.[163]

The Eucharist and Torture

So what? Why does unity matter? What is at stake? One might be tempted to claim that the unity described in this chapter is little more than an abstraction, or irrelevant to the lives of the average Christian. It is not only relevant, but unity, in certain cases, is a matter of life and death. In *Torture and Eucharist*, theologian William T. Cavanaugh offers an example of how consequential unity is. Cavanaugh details how the Augusto Pinochet regime in Chile used torture to dismantle social bodies that threatened its power. "Torture," says he, "is a kind of perverted liturgy, a ritual act which organizes bodies in the society into a collective performance, not of true community, but of an atomized aggregate of mutually suspicious individuals. Just as liturgy is not merely 'spiritual' formation which then must be applied to the physical world, torture is not a merely physical assault on bodies but a formation of a social imagination."[164] The Eucharist, he says, is the answer to this atomization. It is "the church's 'counter-politics' to the politics of torture."[165]

Pinochet toppled the government of Salvador Allende in a bloody military coup. Rather than surrendering, Allende shot himself. As president, Pinochet reversed the Marxist policies of Allende, and instituted a variety of free-market policies, including privatizing many state-owned businesses, creating a central bank, and privatizing the social security system. He also banned political parties, dissolved the Congress, abolished the Constitution, censored the press, outlawed labor strikes and trade unions, and purged from universities faculty members suspected to be liberals.

Torture largely was carried out by the DINA (*Dirección de Inteligencia Nacional*), a centralized agency established in 1974 comprised of members from all branches of the military. Its stated purpose was to gather intelligence, but it also executed clandestine operations.[166] The atrocities were often perpetrated in secret torture centers around the country, such as the Villa Grimaldi, which was the bureaucratic headquarters of the BIM (*Brigada de Inteligencia Metropolitana*), the Santiago branch of the DINA. Sympathizers of Allende's government, members of banned political parties, unionists, church activists, community organizers, protesters, and possible associates of any of these groups were tortured on the "grill" while copyists took dictation of forced confessions offered under unspeakable pain.[167]

The Pinochet regime rarely tortured to obtain useful information. Torturers, moreover, stopped torturing before the victim died because they did not want to create martyrs. Throughout Christian history, the public witness of martyrs strengthened the Church as a body that resisted the machinations of the state. "The Pinochet regime," Cavanaugh says, "had learned the lessons of the [Roman] Coliseum all too well."[168] According to a 2004 official government commissioned report, over 27,000 people were tortured during Pinochet's reign.[169]

Torture first was a manifestation of state power over the individual body that was intended to humiliate the victims. The unbearable pain broke the wills of most (if not all), causing them to confess their humiliation, and to betray their cause and companions. Second, torture rendered the victims unable to resist the interrogator. Rather than extracting true information from the victims, the interrogator would be able to extract any information—true or false—that the interrogator wanted to hear. Third, victims, broken by physical and psychological pain, would replace their own understanding of reality with whatever reality the state wanted the victims to imagine.[170]

The regime's acts of systematic fear and torture were not intended as exertions of power exclusively over individual bodies but as manifestations of state power over entire social bodies.[171] When released from the torture chamber, victims would take the pain, wounds, humiliation, trauma, scars, and (most importantly) isolation back into society, and reproduce it there. "Torture," Cavanaugh tells us, "breaks down collective links and makes of its victims isolated monads. Victims then reproduce the same dynamic in society itself, with the net result that all social bodies which would rival the state are disintegrated and disappeared."[172] In other words, non-state social bodies (such as the Church) that could resist Pinochet could be fragmented because torture dissolves bonds of kinship, leaving first the victim and then society as a whole powerless against the regime's ambitions.

The Body of Christ in Chile responded to this torture in three eucharistic ways. The first was to excommunicate those who tortured. Excommunication, a means of correction reserved for the rarest instances, was used for several reasons. It was viewed as necessary by many bishops and lay people because torture harmed not only the dignity of individual persons, but the common good, and damaged the ecclesial unity signified by Communion. It was automatic for any who participated in, incited, solicited, or ordered torture, or were in a position to stop torture but failed to do so. Excommunication also reveals, makes visible, and recognizes the disunity within the Christian community caused by Christian torturers who tortured Christian victims. In 1980, seven Chilean bishops excommunicated torturers in their dioceses.[173]

Excommunication was not a perfect solution, however. No specific torturers were ever publicly excommunicated by the bishops in Chile because the regime kept secret the names of the perpetrators. Moreover, bishops disagreed among themselves if excommunication was the correct discipline for four reasons: some thought excommunication was outdated; others believed they did not have definitive proof of the torture; still others were afraid that the regime would only become more vicious; while some thought the lack of unanimity among the bishops rendered excommunication divisive. Pinochet himself was never publicly excommunicated despite a public letter in 1987 by 150 priests, nuns, and laity who called for the bishops to do so.[174]

The Church in Chile, after the regime outlawed social organizations shortly after the coup, also responded by organizing the COPACHI (Committee of Cooperation for Peace in Chile) and then the Vicariate of Solidarity. COPACHI offered legal assistance to tortured victims, laborers who lost their jobs and now could not appeal to any organized unions, and students and professors who had been banned from the universities. It also established a variety of social programs, health clinics, youth groups, groups for relatives of political prisoners, alcohol support groups, and other base groups. After Pinochet forced COPACHI to shut down, Cardinal Raúl Silva Henriquez of Santiago created the Vicariate of Solidarity in 1976 as a Vicariate of the Catholic Church, which gave it official ecclesial protections. The Vicariate, which swiftly established offices in every diocese in Chile, offered similar legal and social programs as COPACHI, but also offered programs like nutritional and educational assistance. At the time, COPACHI and the Vicariate of Solidarity were the only viable societal field hospitals for Chilean society.[175]

Neither COPACHI nor the Vicariate of Solidarity should be viewed simply as social welfare services similar to those non-governmental agencies. Their efforts should be understood rather as work that constitutes a social body—of "knitting people back together."[176] This is not a constitution merely of the body politic, however; it is the constitution of the body of Christ, which, as we have seen throughout this chapter, is the work of the Eucharist:

> The work of the [Vicariate of Solidarity] is Eucharistic because it is not just any body which the church realizes, but the body of Christ. Christ's true body is enacted here by the incarnation of the church in the bodies of the poor. The true body of Christ is the suffering body, the destitute body, the body which is tortured and sacrificed. The church is the body of Christ because it performs an *anamnesis* [memorial] of Christ's sacrifice, suffering in its own flesh the afflictions taken on by Christ. In the church's communities of solidarity, the poor are fed by Christ, but insofar as they become Christ's body, they also become food for others. The Eucharist reveals the true meaning of solidarity. It should come as no surprise that reception of the Eucharist increased dramatically among the poor during the military dictatorship.[177]

The eucharistic work of COPACHI and the Vicariate of Solidarity made the body of Christ in Chile real as "a counter-discipline to the discipline of the state."[178]

The third response was the Movement against Torture, which began in 1983 when a group of seventy priests, nuns, and laypeople protested in front of one of the regime's clandestine prisons by raising a banner that read, "A man is being tortured here." Twenty-four of them were arrested. The Movement later was renamed the Sebastián Acevedo Movement after two children of a manual laborer by that name were taken by the government. Three days later, still not knowing where his children were, Acevedo sat in front of a cross at the cathedral of Concepción and set himself on fire. Acevedo demanded that the government return his children, and prayed "Lord, forgive them, and forgive me too for this sacrifice."[179]

The Sebastián Acevedo Movement was not a standard form of protest. It is better described as "street liturgy."[180] The protesters performed public rituals of solidarity with those who were tortured and oppressed by Pinochet. They would choose places to protest that were charged with symbolic meaning, such as torture centers, court houses, governmental buildings, and media offices. The protesters would gather at these locations at specifically planned days and times. They would unfold banners, distribute fliers, disrupt traffic, sing songs, and pray litanies of prophetic protest that publicly named the government's evil. Sometimes, the protesters would be able to melt back into the crowd after performing the short liturgies. Often, however, the authorities would arrest them quickly before they had finished.

These liturgies of protest accomplished more than simply voicing injustices. They made visible the invisible atrocities that were hidden in nondescript buildings, and they made public what the government wanted to keep private. The protesters named the nameless victims, the locations of torture, the terrible acts, and even many of the torturers. The protesters themselves were then violently attacked by governmental forces with tear gas, water hoses, and batons, and were taken away to prison. This, too, was part of the protesters' plan for unmasking the horror. The street liturgy manifests the regime's cruelty, and it is "designed to make the tortured body, which has been disappeared by the state, miraculously appear in the bodies of the protesters."[181]

Chapter Six

The Eucharist and Social Justice

If I, therefore, the master and teacher, have washed your feet, you ought to wash one another's feet.

Jesus, at the Last Supper

Introduction

The phrase "social justice" has become commonplace in current public discourse. Predictably, evacuated of its substantive meaning, it has become politicized and little more than a weapon in the never-ending "culture wars" played out in both the legacy and social media. In the Catholic tradition, social justice is not a newfangled trend to be worn as a badge to signal virtue. Rather, from the beginning it has been integral to the life of the People of God, but unfortunately is our "best kept secret."[182] It is important not only to understand what authentic Catholic social justice is and what it is not, but to embrace it unashamedly as an essential part of Christian life.

In the earlier chapter on deification, we saw that reception of the Eucharist yields what Benedict XVI calls an internal "progressive transfiguration" that forms us more closely to Christ by allowing us to participate in his divine life. In other words, if we cooperate with God's grace, the Eucharist more deeply strengthens the "vertical" relationship between us and God, which then transforms our entire being. As we shall see presently, receiving the Eucharist also strengthens the "horizontal" relationship between us and our neighbor.[183] In other words, being more conformed to the heart, mind, and will of Christ by the Eucharist redirects our lives outward—especially toward those who are most in need.

This chapter first will review the Catholic definition of social justice, which differs from a secular vision of justice. Catholic social justice is not only about establishing a rightly ordered society; it is also about living holy lives in response to the gospel call. It emphasizes the dignity of the human person created in the image and likeness of God, marriage, family, social participation, the protection of human rights (especially the fundamental right to life), the fulfillment of familial and societal responsibilities, the option for the poor and marginalized, the rights of workers, human solidarity, and stewardship of the gift of creation. We then will see how a life grounded in the Eucharist flows into a life that works for justice. Finally, we will explore the example of Sara Miles, a self-described unlikely convert to Christianity, whose unexpected experience with Communion radically reoriented her entire life and led her to respond to Jesus' command to "feed my sheep" (Jn 21:15-19) by establishing a unique food pantry.

The Catholic Definition of Social Justice

An important document that describes authentic Catholic social justice is the "Seven Themes of Catholic Social Teaching" (hereafter "Seven Themes") by the United States Conference of Catholic Bishops (USCCB). "Seven Themes" begins with a short but theologically dense definition of social justice: "The Church's social teaching is a rich treasure of wisdom about building a just society and living lives of holiness amidst the challenges of modern society."[184] Four points from this sentence deserve explanation.

The first is that the Church's teaching on social justice is a rich treasure of "wisdom." Wisdom (*sapientia*) here is understood most clearly by contrasting it with "knowledge" (*scientia*). For Augustine, wisdom is "concerned with the intellectual cognizance of eternal things," whereas knowledge is the "rational cognizance of temporal things."[185] These general definitions can apply in countless ways, but we can apply his definitions to mean that social justice does not have its end in understanding and creating a utopia here in this life (temporal things), but ultimately in understanding God (eternal things).

The second claim is that social justice is about "building a just society." In the West, the search for a definition of justice has been going on for centuries. The most famous investigation is Plato's *Republic*, a text commonly read in undergraduate philosophy classes. In it, Socrates and his interlocutors investigate what justice looks like both in society and the individual.[186] Christian philosophers and theologians, too, have investigated the question of justice. Most would assent to Thomas Aquinas's definition that justice "is a habit whereby a man renders to each one his due by a constant and perpetual will."[187] Generally applied, this means that a society is just if it treats each individual as a child of God, rather than a means to an end, an object of use, nothing more than a consumer of goods and services, or a tool for the state or the free market.

Third, social justice is ordered toward "living lives of holiness," which can be understood best in light of the "universal call to holiness" by the Second Vatican Council's document *Lumen Gentium*.[188] Prior to Vatican II, two tiers had developed in Catholicism. The first, those whom we might call "professional Catholics," were the priests, nuns, brothers, and sisters who were understood to be called to a higher moral standard, whereas "amateur Catholics," as we might call them, were called to work in the world, have families, go to Mass every week, donate generously, and be good people, but were not expected to live heroic lives of virtue. Vatican II's call to holiness critiqued this hierarchy, claiming that all Catholics are called to sanctity regardless of vocation. "It is therefore quite clear," *Lumen Gen-*

tium insists, "that all Christians in whatever state or walk in life are called to the fullness of Christian life and to the perfection of charity, and this holiness is conducive to a more human way of living even in society here on earth. In order to reach this perfection, the faithful should use the strength dealt out to them by Christ's gift, so that, following in his footsteps and conformed to his image, doing the will of God in everything, they may wholeheartedly devote themselves to the glory of God and to the service of their neighbor."[189]

Fourth, the pursuits of justice and holiness are impeded by the "challenges of modern society." These numerous challenges cannot all be listed here, but attentive Catholics witness them daily. *Gaudium et Spes*, perhaps the most important document from Vatican II, outlines many of these challenges of the "modern dilemma":[190] rapid social, scientific, and technological changes; an increase in power without the corresponding control of that power for the benefit of humanity; uncertainty; ongoing poverty for many amid a wealthy few; illiteracy; social and psychological slavery; bitter political, social, and economic divisions; racial and ideological antagonism; the specter of nuclear annihilation; an inability to agree on what words mean; material progress without a corresponding spiritual progress; the accelerated pace of history; changes in traditional social relationships; a growing industrial economy that challenges centuries-old social practices; urbanization; unforeseen chain reactions in the wake of new forms of media; increased immigration; the breakdown of personal relationships; questioning moral values; a decline in religious observance; and increasing awareness of inequalities, to name a few.[191]

In another document, "Communities of Salt and Light," the bishops explain that "The most important setting for the Church's social teaching is ... in prayer and worship, especially gathered around the altar for the Eucharist. It is in the liturgy that we find the fundamental direction, motivation, and strength for social ministry."[192] Although the "Seven Themes" document does not refer directly to the Eucharist, the life of a Eucharistic "community of salt and light" is manifested in these themes.

Seven Themes of Catholic Social Justice

The first of the "Seven Themes" concerns the "Life and Dignity of the Human Person":

> The Catholic Church proclaims that human life is sacred and that the dignity of the human person is the foundation of a moral vision for society. This belief is the foundation of all the principles of our social teaching. In our society, human life is under direct attack from abortion and euthanasia. The value of human life is being threatened by cloning, embryonic stem cell research, and the use of the death penalty. The intentional targeting of civilians in war or terrorist attacks is always wrong. Catholic teaching also calls on us to work to avoid war. Nations must protect the right to life by finding increasingly effective ways to prevent conflicts and resolve them by peaceful means. We believe that every person is precious, that people are more important than things, and that the measure of every institution is whether it threatens or enhances the life and dignity of the human person.[193]

On the first day of class, I always tell my students that all the social and moral teachings of the Catholic Church come out of one foundational theme: the dignity of the human person.[194] Why does the Catholic Church oppose abortion? Because abortion is an offense against the dignity of the human person. Why does the Catholic Church oppose the death penalty? Because the death penalty is an offense against the dignity of the human person. Why does the Catholic Church oppose euthanasia? Because euthanasia is an offense against the dignity of the human person. Why does the Catholic Church oppose human trafficking? Because human trafficking is an offense against the dignity of the human person. In short, the principle of dignity guides every Church teaching concerning the human person.

For Catholics, the dignity of the human person is grounded in divine revelation. In an earlier chapter, we saw that human beings are qualitatively different from the rest of creation because God created them in the Creator's image and likeness (Gn 1:26-27). We discussed how these verses suggest that if God, who is a communion of three persons, has created human beings in his image and likeness, we must conclude that we are also created for communion. These are also the most important biblical verses pointing to the sacredness of humanity. If God, who is sacred (Is 6:3), created us in his image and likeness, then we, too, are sacred (1 Cor 3:16-17).[195]

The second theme is the "Call to Family, Community, and Participation":

> The person is not only sacred but also social. How we organize our society—in economics and politics, in law and policy—directly affects human dignity and the capacity of individuals to grow in community. Marriage and the family are the central social institutions that must be supported and strengthened, not undermined. We believe people have a right and a duty to participate in society, seeking together the common good and well-being of all, especially the poor and vulnerable.[196]

In his post-synodal apostolic exhortation *Familaris Consortio*, Pope John Paul II describes the nature of marriage; the identity, mission, and tasks of the family; the challenges and problems families face today; and, most importantly for our purposes, the role of the family in society. Following Vatican II, John Paul II proclaimed that "the family is the first and vital cell of society."[197]

The foundation of the family is the married couple. In the eyes of secular culture, two people get married for their own personal flourishing. According to John Paul II and the Catholic intellectual tradition, however, marriage is a sacrament primarily for the procreation and education of children (Gen 1:28), not a tool for individual fulfillment.[198] The education of children certainly includes basic skills such as how to brush their teeth and tie their shoelaces. But from a Catholic perspective, it is more concerned with forming the human person "in the pursuit of his ultimate end and of the good of societies of which, as man, he is a member."[199] As children grow into adulthood, their first (and arguably most important) formation is the lesson of love.[200] As children grow, they absorb God's lessons of truth, goodness, and moral principles from their parents[201] They develop their gifts, become aware of their inherent dignity, and prepare for the grand adventure of life that God has prepared for them.[202] They become aware of the spiritual patrimony of the Tradition, and become initiated into their cultural heritage, while coming to understand their role in the community.[203]

As an intimate community of life and love, the family finds its ultimate fulfillment in the Kingdom of God. It is a divine institution—the first natural society and a prototype for every other social order.[204] The family's mission to guard, reveal, and communicate love is grounded in and reveals God's love for all humanity.[205] To carry out its mission, the family must accomplish four tasks: (1) to form and develop an authentic community of persons (husband and wife, parents and children, relatives) who live with fidelity the reality of communion;[206] (2) through procreation, to transmit the divine image from generation to generation;[207] (3) to help develop society by modeling and encouraging respect, justice, and love within the family;[208] (4) to share in the life and mission of the Church by building up the Kingdom of God in history.[209]

In recent decades, a myriad of changes in our society and in the family itself have caused a crisis in the domestic Church:[210] increased social acceptance of divorce; the proliferation of second, third, and even fourth marriages; an increase in civil (contractual) marriage disconnected from ecclesial (sacramental) understanding of marriage; a disconnect between marriage and a living faith; a rejection of the morality that demarcates and promotes a truly human sexuality within marriage; an unwillingness to surrender individual independence; a warped conception of how authority is exercised between parents and children; abortion; sterilization; and a contraceptive mindset.[211] Destructive changes and pressures from outside the family have also done incalculable damage.[212] Mass media, movies, television programs, music, and literature, for example, deliberately obscure the fundamental values of the family.[213]

Since 1981 when John Paul II compiled his list, a number of other dangers have torn the fabric of marriage, including the increase in divorce caused by the rise of social media,[214] the change in definition of marriage most clearly seen in the Supreme Court's 2015 *Obergefell v. Hodges* decision that federally allows homosexual marriage in the United States,[215] the proliferation of civil laws that provide an easier path towards divorce, and societal factors such as economic pressures and pornography that diminish the desire in both men and women to get married.

The third theme of Catholic social justice is "Rights and Responsibilities:"

> The Catholic tradition teaches that human dignity can be protected and a healthy community can be achieved only if human rights are protected and responsibilities are met. Therefore, every person has a fundamental right to life and a right to those things required for human decency. Corresponding to these rights are duties and responsibilities—to one another, to our families, and to the larger society.[216]

It may seem obvious that the human person has an inherent right to life, but the secular world today rejects it. In his encyclical *Evangelium Vitae*, John Paul II prophetically critiqued the "culture of death" that seeks every opportunity to violate the right to life and the dignity of the human person. He defines the "culture of death" as being "actively fostered by powerful cultural, economic and political currents which encourage an idea of society excessively concerned with efficiency."[217] This obsession with efficiency warps our vision of the value of the human person, especially the value of women, children, the sick, the suffering, and the elderly. It devalues our inherent sacredness, grounding human worth in contingent values such as usefulness defined by what one has, can do, and can produce,[218] exceptional strength, intelligence, beauty, and health,[219] and the ability to communicate.[220] Those who cannot meet these standards because of illness, age, lack of opportunities, lack of education, or disability (among other reasons) become subject to "the will of the stronger part"[221] that determines the fate of the weaker part.

This determination "of the stronger part" manifests itself in a number of ways. Experimenting with human embryos and fetuses in the hope of future health treatments, for example, gives priority to therapeutic usefulness, disregarding the inherent worth of the unborn.[222] These increasingly common biomedical experiments view the human person as a mere means to the more important ends of scientific discovery, the preservation of those who offer social utility, or, most scandalously, profit.[223]

The fourth of the seven themes of Catholic social justice is the "Option for the Poor and Vulnerable." "A basic moral test," the "Seven Themes" states, "is how our most vulnerable members are faring. In a society marred by deepening divisions between rich and poor, our tradition recalls the story of the Last Judgment (Mt 25:31-46) and instructs us to put the needs of the poor and vulnerable first."[224] A notable American example of putting the needs of the poor and vulnerable first in is the Catholic Worker Movement, co-founded by Peter Maurin, the visionary who "left people agitated,"[225] and Dorothy Day, the Communist convert to Catholicism.[226]

Maurin envisioned the Catholic Worker as having three parts.[227] The first was a Catholic newspaper "for the clarification of thought."[228] In order to act well, one must study and think clearly, otherwise one's actions will become disordered. *The Catholic Worker* newspaper encourages dialogue that leads to such clarity. In May 1933, the first issue was sold in Union Square for one penny, the price that remains to this day.[229] Under Day's direction, the newspaper often focused on labor news, including working conditions, wages, and labor strikes.[230]

Maurin's vision also included establishing houses of hospitality. These houses accepted everyone in need. Based on similar "houses" in medieval Europe,[231] they offered not only the basic material necessities of life such as food, clothing, and shelter, but also opportunities to elevate the soul through prayer.[232] The first house opened while the second issue of the newspaper was being drafted. It did not begin with a mission statement or a set of "best practices." A pregnant unemployed textile worker simply went into the kitchen and began preparing meals for the homeless who had begun congregating on Fifteenth Street.[233] Over time, similar houses began independently all over the country, offering their communities hospitality in different ways depending on need.[234]

A farming commune and agronomic university was the third part of the Catholic Worker Movement. According to Maurin, it would offer "the solution to all the ills of the world, unemployment, delinquency, destitute old age, man's rootlessness, lack of room for growing families, and hunger."[235] In light of overcrowded cities and industrialized machines that had displaced workers, he proposed a return to the land.[236] Workers and scholars would benefit by living and working together, furthering their "clarification of thought" and allowing both groups to participate in the dignity of work. In 1935 on Staten Island, the first Catholic Worker commune opened. It was so small that they affectionately called it the "garden commune."[237] The following year, on the feast day of St. Isidore the Farmer, they acquired twenty-eight acres of land three miles outside of Easton, Pennsylvania and named it Maryfarm. They began constructing dormitories, accepting the destitute, tilling the land, planting crops, even buying a cow they named "Rosie." Like the houses of hospitality, farming communes and agronomic universities began appearing all over the country.[238]

The fifth theme of Catholic social justice is "The Dignity of Work and the Rights of Workers":

> The economy must serve people, not the other way around. Work is more than a way to make a living; it is a form of continuing participation in God's creation. If the dignity of work is to be protected, then the basic rights of workers must be respected—the right to productive work, to decent and fair wages, to the organization and joining of unions, to private property, and to economic initiative.[239]

In his encyclical *Laborem Exercens,* published in 1981 in honor of the ninetieth anniversary of Pope Leo XIII's *Rerum Novarum,* John Paul II offers a Catholic analysis of work. Work, the pope says, is part of human nature.[240] It is not a punishment for the sin of our first parents (Gen 3:17).[241] Therefore, work itself is good when it is rightly ordered. In our capitalist society today, work becomes disordered when the human person becomes an object of use for the sake of profit. Work should never be the master of humanity. John Paul II insists that "work is 'for man' and not man 'for work.'"[242]

Work has dignity and moral value. It is useful as the means for obtaining other goods (material goods, cultural experiences, social experiences). Moreover, work itself, even physical work, can be enjoyable. Many take pleasure in getting their hands dirty building houses, working in a machine shop, or tilling the soil. By expressing and increasing the dignity of the human person, work signifies the uniqueness, worth, and sacredness of humanity. Work transforms and adapts nature to ensure human survival, but on a more profound level it allows each man or woman to achieve "fulfilment as a human being and indeed, in a sense, ... [become] 'more a human being.'"[243]

The sixth of these themes is "Solidarity":

> We are one human family whatever our national, racial, ethnic, economic, and ideological differences. We are our brothers' and sisters' keepers, wherever they may be. Loving our neighbor has global dimensions in a shrinking world. At the core of the virtue of solidarity is the pursuit of justice and peace. Pope Paul VI taught that if you want peace, work for justice. The Gospel calls us to be peacemakers. Our love for all our sisters and brothers demands that we promote peace in a world surrounded by violence and conflict.[244]

Pope Francis explores the themes of solidarity, justice, and peace is his third encyclical, *Fratelli Tutti*. In it, he names several trends that hinder the development of solidarity today, including the "illusion of communication" from social media, the "shameless aggression" from online anonymity, and the "information without corresponding wisdom" that the internet produces.

Over the past several decades, technological advancements, such as the rise of the internet and social media, have allowed unprecedented ways of communicating. However these forms of communication, Francis argues, do not build or strengthen social communities in the long run, but only have the "appearance of sociability."[245] They "tend to disguise and expand"[246] an ever-increasing atomizing individualism because they do not foster the slow cultivation of friendships through "physical gestures, facial expressions, moments of silence, body language and even the smells, the trembling of hands, the blushes and perspiration that speak to us and are a part of human communication."[247] This lack of incarnational encounter—that is, physical interactions that occur only when two or more people are in the same room together—fosters addiction, isolation, stunted growth in interpersonal relationships, and the loss of a sense of the true nature of reality.[248]

The anonymity of social media platforms has manifested a "shameless aggression"[249] similar to what Plato imagined in his mythical Ring of Gyges that allowed the ring bearer, Gyges, to become invisible and do as he pleased, including seducing the wife of a king, and killing the king.[250] By allowing us to remain immune from the consequences of our words and actions, our digital rings of Gyges usher in verbal hostility and violence that tear at the fabric of civility.[251]

Technology companies themselves and other economic interests, moreover, manipulate public discourse by ghettoizing like-minded individuals on the internet, allowing them to avoid healthy dialogue and debate with others of different stripes, leading to echo chambers and, in Francis's words, "fomenting prejudice and hate."[252] Christians, too, participate in this aggression, slandering and defaming other Christians, political figures, and even children.[253]

These technological platforms also produce an avalanche of "information without wisdom"[254] that inhibits focused attention, contemplative reflection, the ability to get to the heart of the matter of any idea and to perceive meaning clearly.[255] "True wisdom," Francis says, "demands an encounter with reality."[256] Technology, however, allows us to avoid reality, to narrow our choices in the news we watch, the goods we consume, and the entertainment we prefer, thereby amplifying our established assumptions and tastes and leading to insularity and lack of growth. This mentality can lead to interacting only with the people and lived experiences that suit our tastes, avoiding anyone or anything that challenges us.[257]

Francis calls Catholics to break out of this technological self-absorption, and to acquire the moral virtue of solidarity that "finds concrete expression in service, which can take a variety of forms in an effort to care for others."[258] Solidarity starts from the place of community, not the individual. Those who act in solidarity recognize that the lives of the many are more important than the needs of the few. They seek to dismantle the unjust structures that cause poverty, inequality, unemployment, the denial of rights, and to oppose the injustice of the "empire of money."[259] No matter what form service takes, at root it manifests itself in caring for the most vulnerable. It treats the bodies and souls of those in need with authentic human encounters, rather than with anonymous donations, or limp words of encouragement. Those who are loved, of course, receive the care and attention they need, but those who love also are changed when they set aside their own desires and pursuits for the good of others.[260]

The seventh theme of Catholic social justice is "Care for God's Creation." "We show our respect for the Creator by our stewardship of creation. Care for the earth is not just an Earth Day slogan, it is a requirement of our faith. We are called to protect people and the planet, living our faith in relationship with all God's creation. This environmental challenge has fundamental moral and ethical dimensions that cannot be ignored."[261] In his 2015 encyclical *Laudato Si'*, Francis offers a comprehensive vision of Catholic environmentalism. Like *Fratelli Tutti,* which begins by naming several contemporary problems that prevent solidarity, his wide-ranging text on the environment begins with a description of several problems causing devastation to our common home, including the "throwaway culture," and the "issue of water."

Francis notes that pollution finds its way into everyone's daily life, leaving "the earth, our home to look more and more like an immense pile of filth."[262] Although a number of domestic and industrial factors cause pollution, a "throwaway culture" mentality—much like John Paul II's "culture of death"—deems what is not "useful" to be disposable: material goods, the planet, and even human beings.[263] In such a mentality, he elaborates elsewhere, "Everything has a price, everything can be bought, everything is negotiable. This way of thinking has room only for a select few, while it discards all those who are 'unproductive,' unsuitable or unworthy, since clearly those people don't 'add up.'"[264] We can reverse the environmental damage to the air we breathe and the soil we cultivate only if we first reverse this dismissive cultural attitude and view our land not as a resource to be exploited and exhausted, but as a divine gift.

Francis singles out water pollution and scarcity as fundamental problems because water is essential for life. Clean and accessible water, he says, is a basic and universal right necessary for other rights.[265] Today, the demand for water outpaces supply, especially in densely populated cities. In rural or undeveloped areas, water scarcity or droughts often limit agricultural production.[266] Major corporations have commodified the resource, allowing the invisible hand of the market to determine how the limited water supply is allocated.[267] Even when water is available, its quality is often unsafe, especially for the poor. Chemicals from mining, farming, and industry often taint underground water sources. Organic and inorganic pollutants disperse throughout the water table, spreading disease and increasing untimely deaths, especially for infants.[268] Although budgets may be limited, societies must ensure a supply of clean water by increasing funds and educating people not to squander this precious resource.[269] If these problems are not addressed, water scarcity will make food and related products more expensive, and, more importantly, will increase violence in the coming century.[270]

Implementing Francis's ideas requires a conversion of heart and mind. A rampant, consumerist mentality has intensified our instability and uncertainty. Self-centeredness and consumptive greed lead to an "empty heart."[271] The desire to fill this emptiness by buying, possessing, and consuming warps our understanding of reality and makes us lose sight of the common good. Without a shared understanding of the common good, social norms can be seen as a threat to our personal needs, and those norms are respected only if they do not interfere with our needs. Conflict between individual needs and the common good can lead to violence and mutual destruction.[272]

Conversion from selfish individualism will allow a new "culture of care" to spread throughout society.[273] This culture of care, marked by commonality and communion, will be grounded in an understanding that we are all brothers and sisters of the same divine father. This way of relating to one another as individuals produces a charity that overflows into all social, political, and economic relationships, into all of creation. Such a "civilization of love"[274] unlocks social and ecological development. Only authentic love ordered toward all created reality can drive new attitudes, strategies, and policies that will stop further environmental damage and allow the world to begin to heal.[275]

The Eucharist and Catholic Social Justice

In a familiar passage from the First Letter of John, the author says that "God is love" (4:8). The original Greek word translated as "love" is *agape*. In the Latin translation of the Bible known as the Vulgate, agape is translated as *caritas*. *Caritas* is usually translated into English either as "love" or "charity" because neither English word fully expresses the original Latin meaning. In the Christian tradition, *caritas* is not defined as "love" in the sense of emotion, although it may be accompanied by emotion. It also is not "charity" in the sense of a donation or financial assistance. As C.S Lewis defines it in *Mere Christianity*, *caritas* "means 'Love, in the Christian sense.' ... It is a state not of the feelings but of the will; that state of the will which we have naturally about ourselves and must learn to have about other people."[276] In other words, love is willing and seeking the good of the other for the sake of the other.

As "the school of active love,"[277] the Eucharist allows us to have the state of will for other people that reflects the state of will we have naturally for ourselves. That is, the Eucharist suffuses us with *caritas,* causing us to will the good of the other not as a means for our own ends but for his or her own sake. When we receive the Eucharist, John Paul II says, "There opens in our souls a real dimension of that unfathomable love that includes everything that God has done and continues to do for us human beings. . . . Together with this unfathomable and free gift, which is charity revealed in its fullest degree in the saving sacrifice of the Son of God, the sacrifice of which the Eucharist is the indelible sign, there also springs up within us a lively response of love. We not only know love; we ourselves begin to love."[278] Because of this infusion, John Paul II titled the Eucharist the "sacrament of love."[279]

If we cooperate with it, *caritas* transforms us to lead lives that strive for justice. At the beginning of *Caritas in Veritate,* Benedict XVI stresses that the *caritas* we receive in the Eucharist cannot be guarded selfishly but must be given away. Most importantly, it must stretch outward in service to those on the margins, especially the poor.[280] "Charity," he insists, "is at the heart of the Church's social doctrine. Every responsibility and every commitment spelt out by that doctrine is derived from charity which, according to the teaching of Jesus, is the synthesis of the entire Law (see Mt 22:36-40). It gives real substance to the personal relationship with God and with neighbour."[281] This "real substance," he says, the "generous engagement in the field of justice and peace,"[282] denounces "inhumane situations in which people starve to death because of injustice and exploitation, and it gives us renewed strength and courage to work tirelessly in the service of the civilization of love."[283]

The most obvious biblical example of how the Eucharist and a life of *caritas* are connected is Jesus washing the feet of his disciples at the Last Supper, the night that Jesus instituted the Eucharist (Jn 13:1-20). "Before the feast of Passover," we are told,

Jesus knew that his hour had come to pass from this world to the Father. He loved his own in the world and he loved them to the end. The devil had already induced Judas, son of Simon the Iscariot, to hand him over. So, during supper, fully aware that the Father had put everything into his power and that he had come from God and was returning to God, he rose from supper and took off his outer garments. He took a towel and tied it around his waist. Then he poured water into a basin and began to wash the disciples' feet and dry them with the towel around his waist. He came to Simon Peter, who said to him, "Master, are you going to wash my feet?" Jesus answered and said to him, "What I am doing, you do not understand now, but you will understand later." Peter said to him, "You will never wash my feet." Jesus answered him, "Unless I wash you, you will have no inheritance with me." Simon Peter said to him, "Master, then not only my feet, but my hands and head as well." Jesus said to him, "Whoever has bathed has no need except to have his feet washed, for he is clean all over; so you are clean, but not all." For he knew who would betray him; for this reason, he said, "Not all of you are clean." (13:1-11)

In antiquity, when people gathered for a meal, they would not sit at a common table but would recline around a room with their feet near each other's faces.[284] In wealthy households, slaves would wash the guests' feet to avoid any unpleasant smells during the meal.[285] When he washed Peter's feet, the "master" (13:13) was doing the work of a slave. Jesus' gesture would have horrified the disciples as a serious transgression and subversion of cultural norms. Masters don't serve. Slaves do.

The message Jesus was trying to send could not have been clearer, although, as usual, he had to spell it out for his disciples:

So when he had washed their feet [and] put his garments back on and reclined at table again, he said to them,

"Do you realize what I have done for you? You call me 'teacher' and 'master,' and rightly so, for indeed I am. If I, therefore, the master and teacher, have washed your feet, you ought to wash one another's feet. I have given you a model to follow, so that as I have done for you, you should also do. Amen, amen, I say to you, no slave is greater than his master nor any messenger greater than the one who sent him. If you understand this, blessed are you if you do it. I am not speaking of all of you. I know those whom I have chosen. But so that the scripture might be fulfilled, 'The one who ate my food has raised his heel against me.' From now on I am telling you before it happens, so that when it happens you may believe that I AM. Amen, amen, I say to you, whoever receives the one I send receives me, and whoever receives me receives the one who sent me." (13:12-20)

He mandates all his followers—those in the Upper Room, and those down through the centuries—to serve each other, regardless of social standing. In offering this model and command during the Last Supper, Jesus clearly intertwines the Sacred Banquet and service, prompting John Paul II to label Jesus as "the teacher of communion and of service."[286]

The liturgy itself also signals the relationship between the Eucharist and service. At the conclusion of Mass, a deacon or the priest dismisses the congregation by saying "Go forth, the Mass is ended," "Go and announce the Gospel of the Lord," "Go in peace, glorifying the Lord by your life," or "Go in peace." When I came into full communion with the Catholic Church, before the change in the English translation of the Mass in 2011, the deacon or priest would announce, "The Mass has ended, go in peace to love and serve the Lord." These might be considered the most important words of the entire Mass because they specify the reason for gathering: we come together not for the sake of prayer itself, but to go out into the world and transform it after we pray.

Consider the Mass like the huddle in a football game. No one watches the game for the huddle, because it is not exciting. However, it is crucial for the flow of the game. The players get together before each play to coordinate their efforts to the same end. The huddle is crucial, but not for its own sake. The play itself is paramount.

In a similar way, the Mass is not for its own sake, but is like a huddle where the People of God come together to get on the same spiritual page. Once the corporate prayer has ended, the action begins. We are called to go out into the world throughout the week and "love and serve the Lord" by loving and serving his people. As Henri Nouwen has said, "Communion, that sacred intimacy with God, is not the final moment of the Eucharistic life. We recognized him [in the breaking of the bread], but that recognition is not just for us to savor or to keep as a secret."[287] We are called to share that intimacy with the world through our love.

Feed My Sheep

In her memoir *Take This Bread: A Radical Conversion*, Sara Miles offers a powerful narrative of a life of charity grounded in her experience of the Eucharist.[288] Before her turn to Christianity through the Episcopal Church, Miles described herself as a "very unlikely convert: a blue-state, secular intellectual; a lesbian; a left-wing journalist with a habit of skepticism."[289] For the first forty years of her life, she had little interest in religion, and no knowledge of Christianity. But after wandering into St. Gregory of Nyssa in San Francisco "with no more than a reporter's habitual curiosity"[290] and receiving Communion for the first time, she was stunned at her encounter. To her surprise, what she would find at the heart of Christianity, she says, is not theological infighting, doctrinal rigidity, outward piety, sexual ethics, or empty ritual, but a radically open tradition grounded in sacraments and service. "I was," Miles recounts, "as the prophet said, hungering and thirsting for righteousness. I found it at the eternal and material core of Christianity: body, blood, bread, wine, poured out freely, shared by all. I discovered a religion rooted in the most ordinary yet subversive practice: a dinner table where everyone is welcome, where the despised and outcasts are honored."[291]

Taking a long walk one Sunday morning, Miles came upon St. Gregory's as she had done many times before. She entered with no interest in becoming a Christian, or, as she framed it in her own mind, "a religious nut."[292] Like many entering a Christian space for the first time, she sat down and hoped no one would notice her. She listened to two cantors in robes chant acapella in harmony. The congregation performed their dizzying liturgical gymnastics of standing, sitting, standing, sitting, and standing and sitting again. They sat in Quaker-esque periods of long silence, then sang together as a body. Although she found the ritual peaceful, "It crossed my mind that this was ridiculous."[293] When the congregation was called to gather around the table, someone put food in her hand and said, "the body of Christ," and gave her a cup, saying "the blood of Christ." "Then," she later recalled, "something outrageous and terrifying happened. Jesus happened to me."[294]

The entire experience made no sense to her. In her mind, she reasonably perceived that she was doing nothing more than eating a piece of bread, something she had done countless times before. Somehow, however, she knew that her rational judgment was incorrect, and that "God, named 'Christ' or 'Jesus,' was real, and in my mouth—utterly short circuited my ability to do anything but cry."[295] But she resisted this, and tried to explain it all away. Could it be, she wondered, that she had become entranced at an emotional level by the music, the architecture, the art, the lighting, and the liturgy? Could it be that standing among all those believers she had been swept up in the moment and momentarily accepted their superstitions? Could it be that after years of sadness built up behind an emotional wall, she had broken through into a space where she could anonymously cry? All these were plausible, but she knew that they could not explain what had actually happened to her: "That impossible word, *Jesus*, lodged in me like a crumb. I said it over and over to myself, as if repetition would help me understand. I had no idea what it meant; I didn't know what to do with it. But it was realer than any thought of mine, or even any subjective emotion: it was as real as the actual taste of the bread and wine. And the word was indisputably in my body now, as if I'd swallowed a radioactive pellet that would outlive my own flesh."[296]

Like the disciples who rejected Jesus' claim of being the Bread of Life (Jn 6:66), the biases against Christianity rose in her, causing her to resist what she knew to be true. Her ignorance of the history and thought of Christianity, along with her lack of any personal connection with Jesus, made it difficult for her to comprehend the scope of meaning of what she had experienced. Her previous lack of interest in reflecting on the existence and nature of God made it difficult for her to perceive the connection between a mysterious and invisible Creator and a Jew from a dusty outpost in an obscure corner of the Roman Empire two thousand years ago. "I couldn't reconcile the experience with anything I knew or had been told. But neither could I go away: for some inexplicable reason, I wanted that bread again. I wanted it all the next day after my first communion, and the next week, and the next. It was a sensation as urgent as physical hunger, pulling me back to the table at St. Gregory's through my fear and confusion."[297]

Miles thought she had lost her mind. For weeks, she wandered in a daze, unable to put into thought or word what had happened within her. In the course of a single day, she would oscillate among a wide range of emotions—confusion, fear, excitement, hunger, and lack of appetite. Each Sunday, she would return to St. Gregory's to receive Communion, and burst into tears. She was filled with dread at the thought of telling her atheist mother, whom she knew would disdainfully dismiss it all. But Miles could not dismiss it. Though her mind told her that the wine came from a jug with a screw top that could be bought in any local grocery store, deep in her bones she knew what was in the cup was something more. "So, then, was it a symbol?" she interrogated herself. "Did the actual wine symbolically represent the imagined blood? No, because when I opened my mouth and swallowed, everything changed. It was real."[298]

What changed most dramatically was how Miles lived her life. Grounded in the Eucharist, she began asking a new set of questions that would produce unexpected answers: "I was tasting a connection between communion and food—between my burgeoning religion and my real life. My first questioning year at church ended with a question whose urgency would propel me into work I'd never imagined: Now that you've taken the bread, what are you going to *do*?"[299] The answer emerged when the dialogue between Jesus and Peter began to haunt her. She kept returning to the moment when Jesus—not for the first time—upended Peter's world. Jesus asked Peter if he loved him, and Peter responded "Yes, Lord, you know that I love you." He then commanded Peter to feed his sheep. A second time, Jesus asked Peter if he loved him, and Peter once again responded "Yes, Lord, you know that I love you." Jesus repeated his command. A third time, Jesus asked Peter if he loved him. Exasperated, Peter said "Lord, you know everything; you know that I love you." Once again, Jesus repeated his command to feed his sheep (Jn 21:15-19). Miles understood that Jesus' command was not for Peter alone, but for all Christians, including her. "It seemed pretty clear," she said, "if I wanted to see God, I could feed people."[300]

Shortly afterwards, she began to visualize what she could do after seeing an advertisement from a local food bank. She decided to start a food pantry, but one unlike any other: not another soulless handout or social-service program, but a different sort of church, one modeled on the Eucharist. She would not require anyone to complete paperwork, produce government identification cards, or fill out questionnaires. Recipients would not need to recite any creeds or hold to specific orthodox doctrines.[301] "It was communion, after all," she said of what she was envisioning, "but with free groceries instead of bread and wine. With the 'everyone' of 'Jesus invites everyone to his table' extended, so that more sinners and outcasts could share the feast. With the literal bread of life served from the same table as the bread of heaven. This is it, I thought, what I'm supposed to do: *Feed my sheep.*"[302]

Unlike other church pantries, hers was not hidden down in the basement. Miles insisted that it be in the same sacred space around the same sacred altar to evidence the connection between the work of the liturgy and the work of love. Each Friday, people from all over San Francisco came for the food, but also for the respect and dignity that they were shown as children of God. Hours before the pantry would open, long lines of the poor, drug addicts, alcoholics, prostitutes, homeless, or mentally ill from every community in the city would assemble. When the time came, small groups were let into the sanctuary to peruse the bounty of vegetables, grains, fruits, and snacks, all reflecting the abundance of the spiritual table. "But as I got to know them," Miles said, "I started to see more clearly how the people who came to the pantry were like me: messed up, often prickly or difficult, yearning for friendship. I saw how they were hungry, the way I was. And then, I had a glimpse of them being like Jesus again: as God, made flesh and blood."[303]

Chapter Seven

The Eucharist as Viaticum

Whoever eats my flesh and drinks my blood has eternal life, and I will raise him on the last day.

Jesus, in the Bread of Life Discourse

Introduction

The Latin word *viaticum* means "provisions for a journey."[304] Since the early Church, it has been used to name the final reception of the Eucharist before death. If not prevented by physical and mental impairment, a dying person receives the Viaticum as sustenance during the transition to the afterlife.[305] Just as physical food is necessary for a serious journey, the spiritual food of the Eucharist is necessary for the even more serious journey beyond this life. In receiving Jesus in the Eucharist, the dying are strengthened, sustained, and safeguarded by the promise of the resurrection.[306] At the point of death, "Christians [are] able to assimilate their dying bodies into Christ's resurrected body, and so begin the transition from a decaying earthly life into an indestructible resurrection life."[307]

Canon Law recommends that the Viaticum be received daily during the days prior to death. Generally, Catholics are allowed to receive the Eucharist once a day. If an unexpected threat of death becomes imminent, however, Catholics may receive the Viaticum again even if they had received it earlier that day.[308] If possible, the dying will receive the Viaticum under both species during Mass, which may be celebrated in the home. If this is impractical, the Viaticum may be received outside of Mass.[309] Usually, a priest will administer the Viaticum, but a deacon or lay person may also bring it to the dying.[310] If Mass is not celebrated, the liturgy for the Viaticum includes an opening rite, confession of sins, reading from Scripture, reaffirmation of the baptismal confession, intercessory prayers, administration of the Eucharist, and a closing rite.[311]

In this chapter, we first will come to a clear understanding of the Christian vision of the body, death, and the afterlife, because the Eucharist as "food for the journey" will make sense only when we understand "who" is on the journey (the body and the soul), the "journey" itself (death), and the "destination" (the resurrection). We will begin by reviewing two schools of thought in the West about the body. The secular view considers the body at best to be a nuisance and at worst evil. Christians, on the other hand, insist that the body, created by God, is good. Then we will examine two views of death. The first considers death to be bad and should be delayed at all costs. Christians, on the other hand, consider death to be good because it frees everyone from the suffering of this life. Next, we will explore two different assumptions about the afterlife. The popular contemporary view holds that there is no afterlife, and so, like a computer being turned off, death ushers in nothingness. Christians, however, believe that after this life there will be a resurrection of the dead in body and soul.

After examining the body, death, and the afterlife, we will examine the "food for the journey" itself. We will see that a parallel *viaticum* already was part of Greek and Roman culture in antiquity. More importantly for Christians, God gave the Israelites "food for the journey" as they wandered in the desert for forty years. In his Bread of Life Discourse (John 6), Jesus elevated the physical nourishment of the manna into spiritual nourishment by proclaiming himself "the true bread from heaven" (Jn 6:32).

The Body

There has always been a strain of thought in the West that has looked suspiciously on the body. In ancient Greece, for example, Diogenes the Cynic believed the body to be worthless after death. He instructed his students that, after his death, they were not to waste their time or energy burying his corpse, nor having a service in his honor. He told them to toss it over the wall of the city. Shocked, they reminded him that if his body were not buried, the birds and animals would devour it. He responded that the animals could not do so if his students would leave him a staff with which to drive away the predators. Perplexed, they asked him how he could drive them away if he were no longer alive. "How am I then injured by those animals," he responded, "if I have no sensation?"[312]

A contemporary of Diogenes, Socrates, believed the soul to be "a helpless prisoner, chained hand and foot in the body."[313] The body is dangerous because it distracts the soul in its pursuit of Truth. The body weighs the soul down with its need for food, and its irrational emotions such as love, desire, and fear, which often lead to wars and revolutions.[314] Socrates claimed that "the soul can reason best when it is free of all distractions such as hearing or sight or pain or pleasure of any kind—that is, when it leaves the body to its own devices."[315] The philosopher's main pursuit must be to "get rid of the body and contemplate things in isolation with the soul in isolation."[316] By doing so, the philosopher prevents the soul from being frustrated by the body.

Contemporary Americans today, even most Christians, maintain this ancient contempt for the body. They dismiss the body as nothing more than a "shell," which is "not the real person." Only the soul is "real," whatever "real" means. The body does not matter. In his care of the dead and the living, poet and undertaker Thomas Lynch has heard such comments for decades. His collection of essays, *The Undertaking: Life Studies from the Dismal Trade*, recounts many such facile analyses. "You hear a lot of it from young clergy," Lynch says, "old family friends, well-intentioned in-laws—folks who are unsettled by the fresh grief of others. You hear it when you bring a mother and a father in for the first sight of their dead daughter, killed in a car wreck or left out to rot by some mannish violence. It is proffered as comfort in the teeth of what is a comfortless situation, consolation to the inconsolable."[317] Although intended to comfort those who loved the deceased, such consolation only increases their suffering.

Christianity has always offered a critique of this pessimistic view of the body. The assertion of the goodness of the body is found in the biblical narratives of creation in Genesis that we mentioned earlier in this book. In the first creation narrative, God creates "the heavens and the earth" (1:1). God continues to create, and then declares the light (1:4), the earth and sea (1:10), the vegetation (1:12), the greater light to govern the day, the lesser light to govern the night (1:16-18), the abundance of living creatures in the water (1:20-21), and every kind of living creature on the earth to be good (1:24-25). When God then makes human beings, he does not explicitly declare them to be good, which Augustine interprets to indicate humanity's incompleteness, a deliberate incompleteness because at some point in the future God intended to make humans more than human.[318] At the end of the narrative, "God looked at everything he had made, and found it very good (1:31)." Christians understand the goodness of "everything" in creation to include the body.

The New Testament also speaks of the goodness of the body. The Gospel of John states, "In the beginning was the Word" (1:1). Over the centuries, the "Word," a translation of the Greek word "*Logos*," has become a nuanced theological term. The Word is understood to be the second person of the Trinity, who—as the Creed states—is "begotten, not made, consubstantial with the Father." In short, the Word "was with God, and the Word was God" (1:1). God, in Jewish and Christian understanding, does not have a body, but the Word "became flesh and made his dwelling among us" (1:14), as we saw earlier. Many followers of Jesus in the first few centuries fought over the meaning of this Gospel claim. The Docetists, for example, claimed that the Word did not assume a real body, but only "seemed" to have one. The New Testament itself, however, affirms more than once that Jesus was fully human, with a body of true flesh and blood. The Second Letter of John, for example, states that "many deceivers have gone out into the world, those who do not acknowledge Jesus as coming in the flesh; such is the deceitful one and the antichrist" (1:7).[319] The good Word could not assume an evil body; hence the material world in general, and the body in particular, must be good. Since Jesus, God himself, did have a body, we can conclude that the body is good.

At each Mass, the Creed begins with a clear declaration: "I believe in one God, the Father almighty, maker of heaven and earth, of all things visible and invisible." Countless volumes have been written over the past seventeen hundred years commenting on almost every word of this Creed. Among other meanings, this theologically dense sentence shapes our view of material reality. If God is the maker of all things visible and invisible, then God is the maker of all material reality, including the body. Moreover, if God is good, then all material reality is good, including the body. No matter how much the body may seem to inhibit the pursuit of truth or how useless the body may seem after death, the body remains good.

Death

Just as the dominant contemporary view of the body as evil conflicts with the Christian view of the body's goodness, the dominant contemporary view of death as evil conflicts with the Christian view of death's goodness.

Since antiquity, death had been understood as a rupture. Obviously, as Socrates described it, physical death allows the "release of the soul from the body."[320] But it is more than a biological event; on multiple levels it encompasses the entire human condition.[321] It causes a rupture in the familial sphere, the social sphere, and the cosmic sphere. It is a breakdown into Chaos, and an inbreaking of mysterious forces beyond human comprehension.

Since the middle of the twentieth century, however, the end-of-life event has become flattened to one dimension that has come to be described as "medicalized death."[322] This new way of thinking about death has multiple features. First, it is an event that takes place in a hospital, rather than in the home where death traditionally had happened.[323]

Second, the shift from home to hospital resulted in more than a shift in place. It also resulted in a shift in perception. Those who, at home, were understood to be dying, now, in the hospital, are understood to be patients. The dying are those who are close to the end of their lives, and have no hope of reversing their fate. Their responsibility is to prepare themselves mentally, emotionally, spiritually, physically, financially, and socially for what everyone acknowledges as inevitable. Patients, on the other hand, are those who are always optimistically viewed as on the road to recovery. The responsibility of the patients themselves, and those surrounding them, is to marshal all their energies toward healing. Any distraction brought on by entertaining thoughts of death could sidetrack the healing process. Death must not be spoken. This shift in mentality evaporated the social and religious rituals meant to provide a narrative of meaning for all those involved.[324]

Third, new medicalized rituals have replaced old rituals. The "congregation of the recovering" don their hospital gowns, gowns that for practical reasons often have no backside, but reflect how these medicalized rituals establish the vulnerability and helplessness of the patients. The medical establishment has replaced the priest as the arbiter of truth and power. The doctor—whose office walls are papered over with degrees, certificates, and awards—is draped in the vestments of the authority of the white lab coat signifying omniscience and omnipotence. The reception of the blood of Christ has been replaced with the drawing of blood for countless medical procedures. The rhythms of the organ, piano, cantor, and choir have been replaced by the rhythms of the electrocardiogram, and the chirping of the ventilator. The collection plate that requests a tithe has been replaced by the medical bill that demands payment of a sum whose provenance is more mysterious than the existence of God.[325]

Fourth, medicalized death has depersonalized the dying process. It has made death a medical event rather than a human event. Death is now diagnosed by brain activity. Even if a person's other organs function properly, medical experts declare death if the approved instruments do not display the brain waves that narrowly define life. Organs that still function are often harvested for the use of those whose brain activity can be detected. Grief, death, and mourning, moreover, are not public events for the members of the community to encounter together, but have been privatized. Public displays of emotion are unseemly, especially in the hospital itself, and anyone betraying this unwritten code of conduct is whisked away by a counselor or social worker to be calmed as quickly as possible.[326]

All these changes have produced in many a heightened anxiety around death and what comes next because a medicalized death does not offer any insight into what happens after brain waves cease. This anxiety, endemic in contemporary society, is exemplified by the author Susan Sontag. Sontag had a lifelong fascination with death. In her travels around the world, she often visited cemeteries, and the human skull she kept on her desk prompted her to contemplate the realities of the body and its terminus. Despite this fascination, Sontag

could not bear to speak of death in general, or her own mortality in particular. According to David Rieff, Sontag's son, to
her "mortality seemed as unjust as murder."[327]

Over the last twenty years of her life, Sontag battled different cancers. In the final months before her death in 2004
because of leukemia, she insisted on risky treatments, even if
they were to take her to the limits of pain.[328] Despite her doctors'
opinion that at her age it would not be effective, she demanded
a bone-marrow transplant. If she did survive, it would leave her
in tremendous pain for the rest of her life. When the transplant
failed, a shocked Sontag begged for even more experimental
therapies. Rieff recounts her reaction when she heard that the
transplant did not work: "'But this means I'm dying,' she kept
saying, flailing her emaciated, abraded arms and pounding
the mattress."[329] At the end, Sontag placed her friends and her
son in a precarious position. Forbidden from speaking of final
things, they could offer her only hopes that they knew were
not true. Unable to come to grips with reality, she did not want
to hear their expressions of affection or acknowledge their
attempts to bring her closure.[330] "She who feared isolation,"
Rieff said, "and had the most terrible difficulties connecting
with people had the loneliest of deaths."[331]

Christianity has always stood athwart such a negative view
of death. In the fourth century, Ambrose of Milan preached
a discourse seven days after the death of his brother, Satyrus,
eloquently describing the goodness of death. The two brothers were very close. When Ambrose was acclaimed bishop
in 374, Satyrus abandoned his own promising civil career to
help Ambrose with the administrative responsibilities that
he faced. As part of his duties, Satyrus journeyed to Africa
to resolve some business disputes. On his way back, the ship
began to sink. Even though he had not yet been baptized (in
late antiquity it was common to delay baptism until the end
of life), he asked some of the Christians on board for a piece
of the Eucharist they had reserved (also a common practice at

the time), which he then wrapped in a piece of cloth and tied around his neck. Afterwards, he immediately sought baptism. Before reaching Italy, he fell ill, recovered, but when he arrived in Rome fell ill again and died there in 378.[332]

Ambrose enumerated multiple reasons why death should be embraced, and life should be held in contempt. "Death," he said in his instruction, "is not only not an evil, but is even a good thing"[333] because "death is a gain and life a penalty."[334] Everyone dies. Death, he explained, was not part of God's design for nature, but became natural. Nothing can prevent it.[335] Moreover, death liberates every person from the desolations of this life. At one point or another everyone gets sick, has personal crises, or must experience the death of a loved one. Our own death sets us free from all pain. The sleep of death provides an eternal Sabbath from the toils of life,[336] which no one truly wants to continue.[337] True beatitude cannot happen in the midst of living, and is found fully only when the limits of the body are no more. Even when life is calm, we are always plagued by anxiety to retain what little we have, and the desire for more. Too often do we hope for fleeting moments of pleasure and impermanent realities. When our hopes fail us—as everything in this valley of tears inevitably will fail us—we become directionless and overwhelmed with despair.[338] Death was not introduced by God as a penalty, but as medicine for the penalty that was established because of Adam's sin.[339] Therefore, death, which even Jesus experienced, should be understood as a necessary step towards salvation.[340]

The Afterlife

Reflections about the body and death inevitably lead us to a reflection about the afterlife. Unsurprisingly, the secular vision and the Christian vision of the afterlife are opposed. To demonstrate the secular vision, we will briefly review comments from two well-known public figures, Christopher Hitchens and Stephen Hawking.

The prominent public intellectual Christopher Hitchens, one of the so-called "New Atheists," dismissed belief in the afterlife. His books such as *Hitch 22: A Memoir*, *The Portable Atheist*, and most famously *God Is Not Great: How Religion Poisons Everything* resonated with many who consider religion to be not only a fairy tale, but the scourge of civilization. After Mother Teresa's death, her private letters depicting her previously unknown spiritual turmoil were published. Hitchens criticized her fiercely, calling her a "troubled and miserable lady."[341] Hitchens died of pneumonia, a complication of esophageal cancer that had been diagnosed in 2010.

In a debate on the afterlife that included Sam Harris, Rabbi David Wolpe, and Rabbi Bradley Shavit Artson, Hitchens said that it is not possible to claim with certainty that there is no afterlife since there is no empirical evidence to support the claim. "We [those at the debate] all admit we don't know [if there is an afterlife] . . . because we can't know." Although conceding that in the absence of empirical certainty he must be agnostic about the afterlife, he asserted that he takes no comfort in realizing that after this life nothing awaits. "We [Hitchens and Sam Harris] are not particularly happy with what we proposed, which is overwhelmingly likely that annihilation and extinction await us. It's just the overwhelming weight of evidence seems that way." Later in the debate, Hitchens clarified: "When I speak about annihilation and extinction, I mean just that. I mean, the screen goes blank, and that's it."[342]

Stephen Hawking, one of the most respected physicists of his generation, held the Lucasian Professorship of Mathematics at Cambridge University, a position previously held by Isaac Newton. Hawking was also the rare scientist who became a public intellectual. In 1988 his book, *A Brief History of Time: From the Big Bang to Black Hole*, sold over nine million copies.[343] A 2014 movie, *The Theory of Everything*, dramatized his personal struggles. He even appeared on popular television shows such as *Star Trek: The Next Generation*, *The Simpsons*, and *The Big Bang Theory*.

Over the years, Hawking's comments about ultimate things have garnered international headlines. His 2010 book *The Grand Design* claimed that a creator is not necessary to account for the origin of the universe. With more certitude than Hitchens expressed, Hawking claimed that people who believe in an afterlife are no different than children. "I have lived with the prospect of an early death for the last 49 years," he said in a 2011 interview with *The Guardian* alluding to the motor neuron disease (MND) with which he was diagnosed at the age of twenty-one. "I'm not afraid of death," he continued, "but I'm in no hurry to die. I have so much I want to do first. I regard the brain as a computer which will stop working when its components fail. There is no heaven or afterlife for broken down computers; that is a fairy story for people afraid of the dark."[344] In recent years, his image of human beings as computers that simply stop working when the power shuts off has become an increasingly attractive way of describing death.

Exploring in detail the nuanced and complex Christian teaching on the afterlife is beyond the scope of this book, but the core of this teaching is that both the body and the soul will be resurrected on the last day. This belief, which is proclaimed at the end of the Creed ("I look forward to the resurrection of the dead and the life of the world to come"), is grounded in Jesus' own resurrection. Although the Gospel of John claims that "Jesus did many other signs in the presence of [his] disciples that are not written in this book" (20:30), the New Testament contains only a few stories about Jesus after the crucifixion. All four Gospels, in fact, conclude shortly after the resurrection. Although the Gospels do not say much about the forty days between the resurrection and Christ's ascension into heaven, the stories that we do have emphasize two important points: Jesus was resurrected in the same body that died on the cross, and after the resurrection that body is somehow qualitatively different.

The Gospels emphasize that Jesus was resurrected in the body first by describing him eating food. After Jesus appeared following the resurrection as recounted in Luke, Jesus asked his followers if they had anything to eat. Although they were stunned that he was in their midst, "They gave him a piece of baked fish; he took it and ate it in front of them" (24:41-42).[345] If Jesus had not been resurrected in his body, it would have been impossible and unnecessary for him to eat anything.

More importantly, the Gospels emphasize that his followers physically touched him. In the same story from Luke, Jesus told his followers to "look at my hands and my feet, that it is I myself. Touch me and see" (24:38-39). The most famous story about a disciple touching Jesus' resurrected body concerns Thomas, called Didymus, often known as "Doubting Thomas." After the resurrection, Jesus showed his followers his hands and side and breathed the Holy Spirit on them (Jn 20:19-23), but Thomas was not in the room at that time. When the other disciples told him that they had seen Jesus, he did not believe them. "Unless I see the mark of the nails in his hands and put my finger into the nailmarks, and put my hand into his side," Thomas said obstinately, "I will not believe" (Jn 20:25). A week later, Thomas was with the disciples in the same room and Jesus appeared. Knowing what Thomas had said, Jesus invited him to put his finger in his nailmarks and his side and told him to believe. After doing so, Thomas could only gasp, "My Lord and my God!" (Jn 20:28).

Jesus' body, though physical, has been mysteriously transformed by the resurrection. The Gospels make this clear by showing that his disciples did not recognize him at first. On the road to Emmaus, as discussed in an earlier chapter, two of Jesus' followers did not comprehend who he was when he started walking with them, and only recognized him in the breaking of the bread (Lk 24:16, 31). Immediately afterward in

Jerusalem, as his disciples were discussing what had happened in Emmaus, Jesus appeared; initially they too did not realize who he was, thinking he was a ghost (Lk 24:37). They only recognized him after he allowed them to touch him, because "a ghost does not have flesh and bones as you can see I have" (Lk 24:39). After the resurrection, Mary of Magdala went to the tomb where she wept when she realized that the body of Jesus was missing. Jesus appeared to her, but she did not recognize him, thinking that he was a gardener (Jn 20:15). She only realized her mistake when Jesus called her name (Jn 20:16). After Jesus allowed Thomas to touch him, he appeared again to his disciples as they were fishing on the Sea of Tiberias. When they were out on the water, Jesus appeared on the shore, but they did not recognize him. Only after they had cast their net on the right side of the boat and were unable to pull the net into the boat because of the number of fish did the disciple whom Jesus loved understand that the stranger was Jesus (Jn 21:1-14).

The Gospels also indicate that Jesus' body had been transformed because he would suddenly appear and disappear. After the disciples in Emmaus recognized Jesus in the breaking of the bread, he abruptly "vanished from their sight" (Lk 24:31). When the disciples rushed back to Jerusalem to tell the others, Jesus appeared to them all and said, "Peace be with you" (Lk 24:36). His greeting "startled and terrified" them (Lk 24:37). When Jesus surprised his disciples by standing in their midst, the author heightens the drama with the detail that "the doors were locked" (Jn 20:19). The same detail is mentioned a week later when Jesus appeared to Thomas (Jn 20:26).

The resurrection was not a one-time event of Christ alone but opened the door for the resurrection of the dead (1 Cor 15:12-19). The baptized are grafted onto the one body, the Church (Rom 11:17; 1 Cor 12:12-13), and Christ is the head of the Church (Col 1:18). Whatever happens to the head, happens to the body.[346] The dead, therefore, participate in Christ's resurrection because, as St. Paul claimed, "We were indeed buried with him through baptism into death, so that, just as Christ was raised from the dead by the glory of the Father, we too might live in newness of life" (Rom 6:3-4).

Like Christ's resurrected body, the resurrected dead will have the same bodies as when they died, yet also transformed. In his first letter to the Corinthians, Paul offers general descriptions of the body before the resurrection and after but does not offer a nuanced description of the differences. He likens the body before the resurrection to a seed, or a kernel of wheat (15:37). This description suggests that a seed and a plant in full bloom may not look the same, but there is an undisrupted continuity between the two. He then names the body before the resurrection as "earthly," while after the resurrection it is "heavenly." Both of these bodies have "brightness," but of two different kinds (15:40). The earthly body is "sown corruptible," but the heavenly is "raised incorruptible" (15:42); the earthly is "sown dishonorable," but the heavenly is "raised glorious"; the earthly is "sown weak," but the heavenly is "raised powerful" (15:43); the earthly is "sown a natural body," but the heavenly is "raised a spiritual body" (15:44); the earthly is "mortal," but the heavenly "must clothe itself with immortality" (15:53). This change from the earthly body to the heavenly body, Paul insists, will occur "in an instant, in the blink of an eye, at the last trumpet" (15:52).[347]

Viaticum: Food for the Journey

Christians did not invent the concept of "food for the journey." In Greek and Roman antiquity, it was common for a meal called the *coena viatica* to be offered to friends or family embarking on a long journey. The term also referred to the money, food, and supplies taken on the journey. *Coena viatica* gained an added level of meaning as the toll to be paid as fare to enter the afterlife. At least as far back as the sixth century BC, it was common for money (*viaticum*) to be buried with the deceased as payment to Charon, who ferried those who had received a proper burial over the river Styx.[348] Loved ones would place a small coin, called an *obolos,* in the dead person's mouth—often between the teeth—and a barley cake in one of the hands. These practices were considered necessary for a proper burial.[349]

Christians in the first centuries did not imitate their pagan neighbors in placing the *obolos* in the mouth of the dead person,[350] but there is evidence that the Eucharist sometimes was buried with the deceased for the journey. Like the *obolos,* the Eucharist would be placed with the deceased—in the mouth, or on the chest, or in a sealed bottle.[351] This practice, common from at least the fourth through the seventh century around the Christian world, was declared an abuse of the Eucharist by a number of councils, including one in Hippo in 393. A second abuse condemned by multiple councils was the practice of offering the Eucharist to someone who had already died, especially if the individual did not have the opportunity to receive it prior to death. This was deemed inappropriate by the third Council of Carthage in 398 because Jesus had commanded his followers to "take and eat" (Mt 26:26), which a deceased person cannot do.[352]

"Food for the journey" is also central to the Old Testament. After Moses liberated the Israelites from bondage in Egypt (Ex 2:23 – 15:22), they wandered in the desert until Joshua brought them into the land of Canaan (Jos 3-24). Although freed from slavery, they still grumbled against Moses because they did not have enough water and food. "If only we had died at the Lord's hand in the land of Egypt," they ungratefully whined, "as we sat by our kettles of meat and ate our fill of bread! But you have led us into this wilderness to make this whole assembly die of famine!" (Ex 16:3). Hearing this, the Lord told Moses that he would rain down "bread from heaven" for them (Ex 16:4).

To test them, the Lord had Moses tell the Israelites to collect only enough for one day. On the sixth day, they were to gather twice as much in order to have enough for the Sabbath, when God would not rain down any bread (Ex 16:4-5). Moses was to tell the Israelites that in the evening twilight they would eat meat, and in the morning would have enough bread. Then, they would know that the Lord is their God (Ex 16:9-12). That evening, quail covered the entire camp. The next morning, a layer of dew descended. When it evaporated, fine flakes like hoarfrost covered the ground. When they saw it, the Israelites asked each other "What is this?" which, in Hebrew, is *"man hu."* This is the origin of the word "manna" (Ex 16:13-15).[353] This manna was similar to coriander seeds, white, and tasted like wafers of honey (Ex 16:31).

The Lord commanded them to gather as much as they needed, one omer (about two quarts) for each person. They were not to keep any leftovers for the morning, and those who ignored the command discovered that the manna they kept turned foul and became riddled with worms. The Lord also commanded them to keep an omer of manna so that future generations may witness the food provided to their ancestors as they wandered the desert. At Moses's direction, Aaron filled a jar and placed it before the Lord in front of the Ark of the Covenant (Ex 16:32-34). The Israelites fed on manna for forty years until they settled in the land that had been promised to Abraham (Ex 16:35; Jos 5:10-12).[354]

Any first-century Jew would recognize the parallels between the Lord providing the Israelites with manna in the desert and Jesus' Bread of Life Discourse. Jesus gave this discourse close to the time of Passover when the Israelites commemorated their liberation from slavery and escape into the desert. Leading up to the discourse, Jesus crossed the Sea of Galilee, recalling the Israelites passing through the Red Sea. A large crowd of people followed him since they had seen him heal the sick. Jesus ascended a mountain and sat down with his followers. When he saw the large crowd of about five thousand, he asked Philip where they could buy food for them. Philip replied that two hundred days' wages could not be enough. Andrew, Peter's brother, brought to Jesus a boy who had five barley loaves and two fish. Jesus took the bread, gave thanks, and had them distribute to the crowd as much as they could eat. After everyone had eaten, he told his disciples to gather the leftovers so that nothing would be wasted. They collected twelve wicker baskets full of bread. Recognizing the parallel with Moses's miracle in the desert, the crowd exclaimed, "This is truly the Prophet, the one who is to come into the world" (Jn 6:14). Jesus realized that they wanted to carry him off to make him their king, so he withdrew to be alone (Jn 6:1-15).

The crowd pursued Jesus. Asking for a sign so that they could believe in him, they said "Our ancestors ate manna in the desert, as it is written: 'He gave them bread from heaven to eat'" (Jn 6:31). Jesus responded that it was not Moses who gave them the bread from heaven. "My father," he corrected them, "gives you the true bread from heaven. For the bread of God is that which comes down from heaven and gives life to the world" (Jn 6:32). The crowd then demanded that he give them the bread always. In response Jesus said, "I am the bread of life; whoever comes to me will never hunger, and whoever believes in me will never thirst. But I told you that although you have seen [me], you do not believe" (Jn 6:35-36). The Jews murmured at this, asking, "Is this not Jesus, the son of Joseph? Do we not know his father and mother? Then how can he say, 'I have come down from heaven?'" (Jn 6:41-44). Jesus commanded them to stop murmuring (Jn 6:43). "I am the bread of life," he said at the climax of the discourse. "Your ancestors ate manna in the desert, but they died; this is the bread that comes down from heaven so that one may eat it and not die. I am the living bread that came down from heaven; whoever eats this bread will live forever; and the bread that I will give is my flesh for the life of the world" (Jn 6:48-51). His listeners could not understand. How, they asked, could he give them his flesh to eat? Jesus responded:

Amen, amen, I say to you, unless you eat the flesh of
the Son of Man and drink his blood, you do not have
life within you. Whoever eats my flesh and drinks my
blood has eternal life, and I will raise him on the last
day. For my flesh is true food, and my blood is true
drink. Whoever eats my flesh and drinks my blood
remains in me and I in him. Just as the living Father
sent me and I have life because of the Father, so also
the one who feeds on me will have life because of
me. This is the bread that came down from heaven.
Unlike your ancestors who ate and still died, whoever
eats this bread will live forever. (Jn 6:53-59)

His audience found this so challenging that "many of his
disciples returned to their former way of life and no longer
accompanied him" (Jn 6:66)—the only story in the four
Gospels where followers left Jesus because of his teaching.[355]

In the early Church, the first textual evidence for the
Viaticum can be found in a letter from Dionysius of Alexandria
to Pope Fabius. Dionysius wrote of a dying man named
Serapion, an upright Christian who, because he had succumbed
to pressure to sacrifice to pagan gods, had been ostracized by
the Christian community. On his deathbed, Serapion had
been speechless for three days. On the fourth day, he briefly
recovered and asked his grandson to find a priest to bring him
the Eucharist. Unfortunately, the priest was sick and could not
come. Instead, he gave the boy a small piece of the Eucharist,
told him to steep it in either water or wine, and then to let the
dissolved host drip into Serapion's mouth. Immediately after
receiving the Eucharist, the old man died.[356]

During the medieval period, the Viaticum increasingly
became the norm throughout the Christian world. From at
least the eighth century, it was common practice to withhold
the Eucharist until the very last moment before death. There
also arose an increasing concern that lay people, often family or
friends of the dying, were usually those who gave the Viaticum

to the dying, as in the story of Serapion receiving from his grandson. Many believed that only the ordained should administer it, but the practical problem of having a priest at the bedside at the exact moment before death prohibited restricting the administration of the Viaticum to priests. It was always of the greatest concern that the dying received the Viaticum before the soul departed the body no matter who administered it.[357]

Starting in the twelfth century, an increased reverence for the Eucharist resulted in the Viaticum being administered earlier in the illness to avoid any disrespect of it. The fast prior to receiving the Eucharist began to be enforced strictly, physical limitations which often prevented dying people from doing. This resulted in the Viaticum being administered to the sick—not just those imminently in danger of death. The meaning of the Viaticum as the "food for the journey" to the afterlife increasingly disappeared. Extreme Unction replaced the Viaticum as the final sacrament for the dying. This order became the dominant pattern during the sixteenth century and lasted until Vatican II.[358]

After Vatican II, the Viaticum was returned to its roots. It was placed after Extreme Unction, once again becoming the final sacrament before death. The dying, as well as family and friends at the deathbed, can receive under both species. If possible, the dying should offer a confession of faith that echoes the confession of faith that the parents or godparents spoke if the individual was baptized as an infant, that the individual proclaimed during the Sacrament of Confirmation, and throughout his or her life during Easter. If a priest is not available at the moment of death, a deacon or lay person may offer the Viaticum. The unique formula said to the dying person captures the essence of the Viaticum: "May the Lord Jesus Christ protect you and lead you to eternal life."[359]

Conclusion

Introduction

Since the first century, the Catholic Church has proclaimed the Eucharist to be the real presence of Jesus' body, blood, soul, and divinity. Just as importantly, when Catholics receive and cooperate with the Eucharist, it produces many fruits. We have reviewed six of the most important fruits: the Eucharist collapses time; it allows Catholics today to participate in Jesus' sacrificial offering on the cross; it allows communicants to share in the divine life of Christ; it unites the human family through unity in Christ; it reorients our lives outward toward those on the margins; it assists in the transition from this life to the resurrected life. It now should be clear why the Second Vatican Council describes the Eucharist as the "source and summit"[360] of the Catholic life. Our entire lives should proceed from and lead back to Christ under the appearance of bread and wine.

Real Presence

The Eucharist is the real presence of Jesus. God's presence to his people is demonstrated first in the Old Testament, most importantly in the Tabernacle, in the Temple, and in the Bread of the Presence. It continued in Jesus himself. When the Word became flesh, it "tented" among us (Jn 1:14). In the Gospel of John, Jesus likens himself specifically to the Temple. The Bread of Life Discourse, also in John, attests most explicitly to Jesus' presence in bread, an attestation that echoes the Bread of the Presence in the Temple. The Tradition of the Church also has always echoed these biblical claims. The *Didache*, St. Ignatius of Antioch, St. Thomas Aquinas, and the Council of Trent are just a few of the many voices that have proclaimed Jesus' presence in the Eucharist.

Memory

Alexander Schmemann describes memory as our capacity to "resurrect the past." At the same time, it is the capacity to transport the present into the past. This can be achieved through our many sensory experiences, such as looking at a photograph album or smelling a familiar perfume. All the senses can trigger memories of the past, as all of us have experienced many times.

More than any other means, liturgy brings the past back to life. According to Kevin Irwin, liturgy gives us access to the salvific acts of the past in which we did not participate. It "reiterates and deepens among us what God did," and it draws us into "God's eternal act of salvation, re-creation, and redemption."[361] Moreover, we are able to share in and participate in those saving events from the past.

For Catholics, the Eucharist makes the past saving acts of Jesus real for us today. It brings those acts into the present and allows us to share God's "presence and love with us sacramentally." At the same time, the Eucharist removes us from the temporal order and places us at the feet of Jesus during the night he was betrayed. There, as it did for all his friends, it gives us access to Christ's body, blood, soul, and divinity. It ushers in a "mysterious 'oneness in time' between that *Triduum* and the passage of the centuries," which lets us "take part" in those acts, and "inexhaustibly gain"[362] for us the fruits of the Easter resurrection.

St. Monica's deathbed appeal illustrates this dimension of the Eucharist. Her "one request"—that her sons remember her when they receive the Eucharist—demonstrates her central concern. She wants her sons to remember her at the altar so that, when she is made present to them by memory and Jesus is made present to them by the Eucharist, a spiritual bond of unity would arise among all of them.

Sacrifice

The Eucharist is the re-presentation of the sacrifice of Jesus on the cross. For Jews and Christians, sacrifice means more than simply giving up something for a greater good. It "sets apart" the offeror. It petitions for God's favor. It expresses adoration, is an act of love and worship, and recognizes the finitude and contingency of this world. Sacrifice is an acknowledgement of the lordship of God over all creation and an act of thanksgiving that returns to God a portion of the gifts that God has given. It is also a key way by which God and Israel ratified their covenants. All sacrifices benefit only humanity, as God is not in need of anything. According to Thomas Merton, sacrifice achieves four goals: it gives infinite glory to God, gives God a perfect return of praise and thanksgiving for all God's goodness, offers to God a worthy propitiation for our sins, and obtains all the temporal and spiritual aids which we need to carry out God's will on earth and to come to union with God in heaven.

The most important Jewish sacrifice is Passover, a yearly commemoration of their liberation from slavery in Egypt. When Pharaoh refused to allow the Israelites to leave, the Lord sent down ten plagues—the tenth being the death of every firstborn. To escape this plague, each Israelite family was to sacrifice a lamb and smear the blood of the sacrifice on their lintels and doorposts. Seeing the blood, "the destroyer" would "pass over" their households and spare their firstborn. Once freed, each year the Israelites continued to recall their

Passover by sacrificing a year-old male lamb without any blemish—including none of its bones being broken. As at the original Passover event, some of the animal's blood would be smeared on their lintels and doorposts. After the lamb was sacrificed, its roasted flesh was eaten. Consuming the meat brought the Israelites into communion with each other and renewed their covenant as God's chosen people.

Later, Mosaic Law restricted all sacrifices—including the Passover sacrifice—to the Temple. Offering sacrifice became the special prerogative of priests, who represented the individual or entire community before God. To atone for all the sins of the Israelites, every morning and every evening, priests would sacrifice a pair of year-old unblemished lambs. In addition, five other main sacrifices were offered at the Temple: the burnt offering, the cereal offering, the peace offering, the sin offering, and the guilt offering.

Christians understand that the person of Jesus of Nazareth, and his offering of himself on the cross, is the culmination and integration of all aspects of Jewish sacrifice. He is the realization of the mysterious Suffering Servant described in Isaiah. He is the new unblemished Passover lamb whose bones were not broken. He is the new sacrificial victim, offered on the cross at the same time and on the same day when at the Temple the priests were slaughtering the Passover lambs. Unlike the Passover lambs, however, Jesus' sacrifice is never repeated. Jesus' sacrifice comprised many elements from the five different offerings Jews made at the Temple: he was sacrificed outside of the city, stripped of his clothes, and drained of his blood.

Catholics access Christ's sacrifice on the cross by means of the Eucharist. This becomes most evident at the Last Supper, the night the Eucharist was instituted. At that meal, Jesus connected his impending death with the Jewish sacrificial practice in four ways. First, Jesus claiming his blood to be the "blood of the covenant" (Mt 26:28) brings to mind Moses at the base of Sinai. There, Moses splashed the blood of the sacrificial animal on the altar as well as on the Israelites, saying "This is the blood of the covenant which the Lord has made with you according to all these words" (Ex 24:8). Second, saying that his blood was "poured out" on behalf of many for the forgiveness of sins (Mt 26:27-28) echoes the sin offering at the Temple, when some of the blood of a sacrificed animal was "poured out" at the base of the altar. Third, Jesus "poured out" his blood on behalf of many for the forgiveness of sins, just as the Suffering Servant "poured out" his life "unto death" (Is 53:12). Fourth, the Suffering Servant shall "justify the many" (Is 53:11), and bear "the sins of many" (53:13), just as Jesus' blood was poured out "on behalf of many" (Mt 26:29). The Eucharist, in sum, is the re-presentation or recapitulation today of the same sacrifice as the one on the cross. In this way, Catholics today participate in Jesus' once and for all sacrificial offering.

Deification

The Eucharist transforms the communicant. This transformation, called *theosis* or deification, is the process of entering into communion and union with God by participating in the divine life of Christ. Deification is initiated by grace in this life and reaches its fulfillment after the resurrection. The communicant is not transformed in nature by the divine life of Christ, but is adopted by grace.

Although the Bible itself does not include the word deification, many biblical passages point to this idea. The first, in Genesis, states that human beings are created in the image and likeness of God (1:27). This indicates that human beings reflect God as a communion of persons. We are created for communion—communion with others but, most importantly, communion with God. The second, from Psalm 82, points to Adam, Eve, and the Israelites as sharing in the divine life, but turning away from God through sin. When Christians participate in the divine life of Christ, the effects of the transgressions of our ancestors are reversed. Third, Paul said that Christ became poor so that we may become rich (2 Cor 8:9). This has become known as the "exchange formula" because, in becoming human, Christ exchanged his divinity for our humanity; when we participate in Christ, we exchange our humanity for his divinity. Fourth, the Second Letter of Peter says that "his [Jesus'] divine power has bestowed on us everything that makes for life and devotion, through the knowledge of him who called us by his own glory and power. Through these, he has bestowed on us the precious and very great promises, so that through them you may come to share in the divine nature, after escaping from the corruption that is in the world because of evil desire" (1:3-4). This is the definitive biblical text for deification. Over the centuries, theologians such as Athanasius and Augustine have expanded and developed these biblical passages.

Although every encounter with Christ (especially through the sacraments) leads to spiritual transformation, the Eucharist is the primary and privileged means by which we are transformed. When we receive his body, blood, soul, and divinity Christ is infused in us; this brings forth a number of spiritual fruits, including the forgiveness of venial sins, perseverance against future sins, growth in the cardinal virtues (justice, fortitude, temperance, and prudence) and the theological virtues (faith, hope, and charity), and an increase in sanctity.

Two biblical stories exemplify how an encounter with Christ leads to radical change. As Jesus was passing through Jericho, Zacchaeus, a thieving and traitorous tax collector, wanted to see him. Because he was short—Cyril of Alexandria interprets this to mean that Zacchaeus was spiritually small—Zacchaeus was forced to climb a sycamore tree. Seeing him, Jesus invited himself into Zacchaeus's "house," which represents the tax collector's interior life. Their meeting—presumably over a meal—moved Zacchaeus to give half of his wealth to the poor and to repay fourfold anyone whom he had extorted.

A second biblical story clearly displays the connection between the Eucharist and transformation. Two of Jesus' disciples were on the road to Emmaus, walking away from Jerusalem. When Jesus approached them, they were prevented from recognizing him because, like Zacchaeus, they were spiritually blind. They told the stranger about the crucifixion and the tomb. Jesus admonished them for their foolishness, and explained how the Scriptures predicted the Messiah. Over the evening meal, Jesus "Took bread, said the blessing, broke it, and gave it to them." Only then did they recognize him. After rushing back to Jerusalem, they told the others how Jesus "was made known to them" in the breaking of the bread.

Unity

The Eucharist is the primary means of establishing unity. Joseph Ratzinger describes this unity as "that peace which we—as separate individuals who live beside one another or in conflict with one another—become with Christ and in him, as one organism of self-giving, to live in view of the Resurrection and the new world."[363] Understanding the power of the sacred meal, which is the integrating force that counters the disintegrating force of sin, begins with understanding the power of what Leon Kass calls our "quotidian" meals. As Kass notes, sharing a meal reorders us into a different social space. It removes us from our cares and concerns, commits us to a plan of eating and to a form and formality that requires us to face each other and behave in a particular way. During the meal, wine—when imbibed temperately—provides the social lubricant for a conversation in which shared trust and intimacy revives the soul, allowing us to share our innermost thoughts, hopes, feelings, fears, and aspirations. Conversation then creates or deepens true friendship, grounded in the desire for the good and virtue of the other.

Unity begins by being grafted onto the body of Christ through baptism and is deepened by the Eucharist. As Paul tells us, we become one body because we eat the one loaf. The Eucharist quantitatively constitutes the Church (which is one across culture, time, and space), and qualitatively makes the body grow because it conforms the Church more closely to the image of Christ.

Paul points to a number of ways by which the unity of the Church is witnessed. The integrity of the Church is founded upon the oneness of the truths of the Deposit of Faith. Unlike the contemporary world, which claims that each person defines his or her own truths, Christians receive revealed truth. Paul also points to the reconciliation between Jews and Gentiles through Christ, proclaiming Gentiles to be "coheirs" along with Jews (Eph 3:6). He also indicates that the financial support which different communities across the Mediterranean offer each other signifies the union of the body of Christ. In a similar vein, the Acts of the Apostles notes how those who came to believe because of Peter's speech at Pentecost shared their possessions and lived a communal life. In the second century, St. Ignatius of Antioch insisted that to be united to the Church is to be united in communion with the local bishop.

The significance of unity is best seen in light of the atomization caused by torture. In Chile, the Pinochet regime used torture to demonstrate its power over individual physical bodies, as well as over social bodies that could prophetically critique the state's malevolence. By excommunicating those who exercised torture on behalf of the government, the Church in Chile responded to this wickedness that made visible the disunity of Christians torturing other Christians. The Church created COPACHI and the Vicariate of Solidarity to address Chileans' social needs; but doing so also manifested the body of Christ as a "counter-discipline" to the state. The Movement against Torture that became the Sebastián Acevedo Movement celebrated "street liturgies," public rituals of solidarity that made visible the state's invisible brutalities and brought into the light the barbarism that Pinochet wanted kept in the dark.

Social Justice

The Eucharist leads to a life that seeks justice. Authentic Catholic Social Justice is "a rich treasure of wisdom about building a just society and living lives of holiness amidst the challenges of modern society."[364] It is "wisdom" because it ultimately is a pursuit ordered toward knowing God. It is intent on "building a just society," where justice is understood as "a habit whereby a man renders to each one his due by a constant and perpetual will."[365] A just society respects the dignity of each member as created in the image and likeness of God. Catholic Social Justice also encourages "living lives of holiness." To be "holy" means to be "set apart," especially from the culture that often opposes God and the Church. Building a just society and living lives of holiness are often hindered by the "challenges of modern society," which are legion.

The Catholic social tradition is marked by seven themes. The first, the "Life and Dignity of the Human Person," declares that every human being is inherently sacred. The second is the "Call to Family, Community, and Participation." Marriage and family, the fundamental building blocks of every civilization, become destabilized when undermined by cultural, political, and institutional forces. The third is "Rights and Responsibilities." Every member of a society has certain rights and responsibilities, but fundamental to all rights is the right to life. The fourth, the "Option for the Poor and Vulnerable," emphasizes the necessity of caring for those on the margins. The fifth is the "Dignity of Work and the Rights of Workers." As human beings, workers have inherent value, not merely the monetary value they bring to an employer. The sixth is "Solidarity." We, in fact, are our brothers' and sisters' keepers. The final theme is "Care for God's Creation." God has given us our common home as gift. We are called to be faithful stewards of this gift.

Love, willing and seeking the good of the other for the sake of the other, is the ground of justice. We receive *Caritas*—God himself—when we receive Jesus in the Eucharist. That Love then leads us to love our neighbors. The relationship between the Eucharist and a life of service is most evident in the Gospels when at the Last Supper Jesus, on the same evening that he instituted the Eucharist, washed the feet of his disciples. Jesus, the master and teacher, modeled for us that true love is caring for those on the margins of society. The liturgy, too, calls us to seek justice. At the end of Mass, the priest or deacon charges us to bring the Love we have received in the Eucharist out of the parish for the transformation of the world.

Sara Miles exemplifies how the Eucharist is linked with the search for justice. Without conscious religious or spiritual motivation, she wandered into St. Gregory's in San Francisco and found herself at an altar being given bread and wine that she was told were Jesus of Nazareth. Although she balked intellectually at a claim that obviously could never be true, something deep inside her knew that, in this case, her reasoning was incorrect. Something much grander was at play. For weeks, she felt split between what reason dictated she must accept, and the reality of her experience. Ultimately the hunger she felt again and again to receive prevailed. She also came to see that she wasn't unique because hunger—both spiritual and physical—were all around her. Knowing that both types of hunger are linked, she responded to Jesus' call to put the Love she received into action. She started a weekly food pantry that she envisioned as a different form of liturgy—one that still gathered around the altar but was Eucharist in a different way. It was Eucharist in action.

Viaticum

The Eucharist is "food for the journey" to the afterlife. When a Catholic is dying, the Eucharist strengthens, sustains, and guards the individual on the journey towards the resurrection. Whenever possible, it should be received in the days leading to death; if death looms, the Eucharist may be administered even if it had been received earlier in the day. It may be received under both species, either within the Mass or, if necessary, outside the Mass. The Viaticum may be administered by a priest, deacon, or layperson.

The Viaticum can be understood fully only within the Catholic vision of the goodness of the body, the goodness of death, and the resurrection of both the body and the soul, not just the soul. In Genesis, when God had finished creating, "God looked at everything he had made"—including the body—"and found it very good" (1:31). The Gospel of John reaffirms the goodness of the body in its claim that the Word, the second person of the Trinity, "became flesh and made his dwelling among us" (1:14). God never would have assumed a body if the body were evil. The Creed—in which we proclaim each week that God is the maker of "all things visible and invisible"—also points to the goodness of the body. Since God is good, and God made all things including the body, the body must be good.

Death, as St. Ambrose clearly affirms in the eulogy for his brother Satyrus, is not an evil but a good to be anticipated. Whereas life is a penalty, death is a gain. Although Adam and Eve, our progenitors, were not created to experience death, death has become part of our nature. Neither technological, scientific, nor medical progress can prevent death. Nevertheless, death is good in that it liberates us from all physical, emotional, spiritual, and psychological suffering. It offers eternal rest from the drudgery of this life. God did not usher in death as a penalty for sin, but as a remedy for the penalty of labor that the sin of Adam and Eve brought upon them. Death, an experience that even Jesus experienced, is an important and necessary step towards the resurrection.

The resurrection of the dead is rooted in Jesus' own resurrection. The stories of the risen Jesus emphasize that his resurrected body was the same as it was before the crucifixion. This is indicated by his eating food, and his disciples physically touching him. At the same time, his body was transformed, as indicated by his disciples not being able to recognize him initially. The dead also will be resurrected like Jesus because the baptized are the Body of Christ, with Christ as the head. As the head goes, so goes the body. Since Christ, the head of the Church, is resurrected, so also the body is resurrected. Just as Christ's resurrected body was both the same and transformed, the bodies of the resurrected dead will be the same and transformed. Paul hints that this resurrected body will be heavenly, incorruptible, glorious, powerful, spiritual, and immortal (1 Cor 15:37-52).

Christians did not invent "food for the journey." It was a practice among pagans to offer friends and family who were leaving on a long journey a meal, the *coena viatica*. The term *viaticum* was also used for the toll due to Charon for ferrying those who had received a proper burial across the river Styx.

The Israelites also had their own type of "food for the journey." After they were liberated from slavery in Egypt, they wandered the desert for forty years. God sustained them by sending "bread from heaven" (Ex 16:4) each morning. This "bread," manna, resembled coriander seeds, was white, and tasted like wafers of honey. God ceased sending the Israelites this bread when they finally reached the promised land.

In his Bread of Life Discourse, Jesus grounds his message in this foundational Jewish story of food that sustains physical life, but he ushers in something entirely new. He himself becomes the "true bread from heaven" (Jn 6:32). Over two millennia, Catholics have prioritized this "daily bread" (Mt 6:11), especially for those in danger of imminent death. In the third century, Dionysius of Alexandria wrote to Fabius about a certain Serapion who, before his death, insisted on receiving the Eucharist. In the eighth century, the Viaticum was commonly administered only at the last possible moment before death, but by the twelfth century, due to a growing emphasis on the required fast prior to receiving the Eucharist, the Viaticum began to be administered to the sick and Extreme Unction became the last sacrament prior to death. After Vatican II, the Viaticum again became the privileged and final sacrament before death.

Bibliography

Anonymous. "Didache." In *Early Christian Fathers*, 171-79. New York: Touchstone, 1996.

Aquilina, Mike. *The Mass of the Early Christians*. Second ed. Huntington: Our Sunday Visitor, 2007.

Aristotle. "Nicomachean Ethics." In *Introduction to Aristotle*, edited by Richard McKeon. New York: The Modern Library, 1947.

Athanasius. *On the Incarnation*. Translated by A Religious of C.S.M.V. Crestwood: St. Vladimir's Press, 1953.

Augustine. *The City of God*. Translated by Marcus Dods. New York: Random House, 1950.

Augustine. *The Trinity*. Translated by Edmund Hill. Hyde Park: New City Press, 1991.

Augustine. *Sermons (230-272b)*. Vol. III/7 *The Works of Saint Augustine: A Translation for the 21st Century*. Hyde Park: New City Press, 1993.

Augustine. *On Christian Doctrine*. Translated by D.W. Robertston. Upper Saddle River: Prentice Hall, 1997.

Augustine. *Confessions*. Translated by Henry Chadwick. Oxford: Oxford World Classics, 1998.

Augustine. *Letters: 100-155*. Translated by Boniface Ramsey. *The Works of Saint Augustine: A Translation for the 21st Century*, Edited by Boniface Ramsey. Hyde Park: New City Press, 2003.

Baker-Brian, Nicholas. *Manichaeism: An Ancient Faith Rediscovered*. New York: T&T Clark International, 2011.

Barron, Robert. *Eucharist*. Maryknoll: Orbis Books, 2008.

Barron, Robert. "Bishop Barron on Catholics Misunderstanding the Eucharist." (2019). https://www.youtube.com/watch?v=0yT-GlYCIvks [accessed August 6, 2022].

Benedict XVI. *Sacramentum Caritatis*. Washington, D.C.: United States Conference of Catholic Bishops, 2007.

Benedict XVI. *Caritas in Veritate*. Washington, D.C.: United States Conference of Catholic Bishops, 2009.

Benedict XVI. *Verbum Domini*. Washington, D.C.: The United States Conference of Catholic Bishops, 2010.

Berman, Joshua. *The Temple: Its Symbolism and Meaning Then and Now*. Eugene: Wipf and Stock, 2010.

Blankenhorn, Bernhard. *Bread from Heaven: An Introduction to the Theology of the Eucharist*. Washington, D.C.: The Catholic University of America Press, 2021.

Bouyer, Louis. *Eucharist: Theology and Spirituality of the Eucharistic Prayer*. Translated by Charles Quinn. Notre Dame: University of Notre Dame Press, 1968.

Boyle, Gregory. *Tattoos on the Heart: The Power of Boundless Compassion*. New York: Free Press, 2010.

Bynum, Caroline Walker. *The Resurrection of the Body in Western Christianity, 200-1336*. New York: Columbia University Press, 1995.

Calvin, John. *Institutes of the Christian Religion*. Translated by Ford Lewis Battles. Philadelphia: The Westminster Press, 1960.

Cantalamessa, Raniero. *The Eucharist: Our Sanctification*. Translated by Frances Lonergan Villa. Revised ed. Collegeville: The Liturgical Press, 1993.

Cassian, John. *The Conferences*. Translated by Boniface Ramsey. Vol. 57. Ancient Christian Writers, Edited by John Dillon, Dennis D. McManus, and Walter J. Burghardt. New York: The Newman Press, 1997.

Catholic Church. *Catechism of the Catholic Church*. Vatican: Liberia Editrice Vaticana, 1994.

Cavadini, John. "Eucharistic Exegesis in Augustine's *Confessions*." *Augustinian Studies* 41:1 (2010): 87-108.

Cavanaugh, William. *Torture and Eucharist: Theology, Politics, and the Body of Christ*. Malden: Blackwell Publishing, 1998.

Cavanaugh, William. *Theopolitical Imagination: Discovering the Liturgy as a Political Act in an Age of Consumerism*. New York: Bloomsbury, 2002.

Clark, Gillian. *Monica: An Ordinary Saint*. Oxford: Oxford University Press, 2015.

Council of Trent. *The Canons and Decrees of the Council of Trent.* Translated by H.J. Schroeder. Rockford: Tan Books and Publishers, 1978.

Cyprian of Carthage. "The Epistles of Cyprian." In *Ante-Nicene Fathers: Hippolytus, Cyprian, Caius, Novatian, Appendix,* 5, 275-420. Peabody: Hendrickson Publishers, 2004.

Cyprian of Carthage. "On the Unity of the Church." In *Ante-Nicene Fathers: Hippolytus, Cyprian, Caius, Novatian, Appendix,* 5, 421-29. Peabody: Hendrickson Publishers, 2004.

Cyril of Alexandria. *Commentary of the Gospel of John.* Edited by Joel Elowsky. Westmont: IVP Academic, 2007.

Cyril of Alexandria, "Commentary on Luke, Sermon 127," https://www.tertullian.org/fathers/cyril_on_luke_12_sermons_124_134.htm#SERMON%20CXXVII (accessed May 28, 2021).

Cyril of Jerusalem. "Catechetical Lectures." In *Nicene and Post-Nicene Fathers: Cyril of Jerusalem, Gregory Nazianzen,* 7, 6-157. Peabody: Hendrickson Publishers, 2004.

Day, Dorothy. *Loaves and Fishes: The Inspiring Story of the Catholic Worker Movement.* Maryknoll: Orbis Books, 1997.

Day, Dorothy. *The Long Loneliness: The Autobiography of the Legendary Catholic Social Activist.* New York: HarperOne, 1997.

Dugdale, L.S. *The Lost Art of Dying: Reviving Forgotten Wisdom.* New York: HarperOne, 2020.

Dulles, Avery. "The Death of Jesus as Sacrifice." *Josephinum Journal of Theology* 3, no. 2 (1996): 4-17.

Edersheim, Alfred. *The Temple: Its Ministry and Services.* Updated ed. Peabody: Hendrickson, 1994.

Eusebius of Caesarea. *The History of the Church.* Translated by G.A. Williamson. New York: Penguin, 1989.

Fagerberg, David. "Liturgy and Divinization." In *Called to Be Children of God: The Catholic Theology of Human Deification,* 274-83. San Francisco: Ignatius Press, 2016.

Favale, Abigail. *Into the Deep: An Unlikely Catholic Conversion.* Eugene: Cascade Books, 2018.

Feingold, Lawrence. *The Eucharist: Mystery of Presence, Sacrifice, and Communion*. Steubenville: Emmaus Academic, 2018.

Francis. *Laudato Si'*. Washington, D.C.: United States Conference of Catholic Bishops, 2015.

Francis. *Fratelli Tutti*. Huntington: Our Sunday Visitor, 2020.

Francis. "Pope in Bolivia: No One Needs to Be Discarded," *America Magazine* https://www.americamagazine.org/issue/pope-bo-livia-no-one-needs-be-discarded (accessed October 10, 2021).

Glancy, Jennifer. *Slavery in Early Christianity*. Minneapolis: Fortress Press, 2006.

Greiner, Katherine. "Thirty Years of Born in the USA." In *Daily Theology*, 2021, June 4, 2014.

Grumett, David. *Material Eucharist*. Oxford: Oxford University Press, 2016.

Hahn, Scott. *The Lamb's Supper: The Mass as Heaven on Earth*. New York: Doubleday, 1999.

Hahn, Scott. *Catholic Bible Dictionary*. New York: Doubleday, 2009.

Hahn, Scott. *The Fourth Cup: Unveiling the Mystery of the Last Supper and the Cross*. New York: Image, 2018.

Hannon, James. "Holy Viaticum: A Historical Synopsis and Commentary." The Catholic University of America, 1951.

Harrington, Daniel. *The Church According to the New Testament: What the Wisdom and Witness of Early Christianity Teach Us Today*. Lanham: Rowman & Littlefield Publishers, 2001.

Hawking, Stephen. "Stephen Hawking: 'There Is No Heaven; It's a Fairy Story.'" In *The Guardian*, edited by Ian Sample, 2011.

Hennessy, Kate. *Dorothy Day: The World Will Be Saved by Beauty*. New York: Scribner, 2017.

Hitchens, Christopher. "Hitchens Takes on Mother Teresa." *Newsweek*, August 28, 2007.

Hitchens, Christopher, "Is There an Afterlife? - Christopher Hitchens, Sam Harris, David Wolpe, Bradley Shavit" https://www.youtube.com/watch?v=UjKJ92b9Y04 (accessed February 5, 2022).

Hunter, David. "Books 21 & 22: The End of the Body: Heaven and Hell in the *City of God*." In *The Cambridge Companion* to *Augustine's City of God*, edited by David Meconi, 276-96. Cambridge: Cambridge University Press, 2021.

Ignatius of Antioch. "Epistles." In *Early Christian Fathers*, 87-120. New York: Touchstone, 1996.

Irwin, Kevin. *Models of the Eucharist*. Mahwah: Paulist Press, 2005.

John Paul II. *Dominicae Cenae*. Boston: Pauline Books and Media, 1980.

John Paul II. *Evangelium Vitae*. Boston: Pauline Books and Media, 1995.

John Paul II. "Laborem Exercens." In *Catholic Social Thought: The Documentary Heritage*, edited by David and Thomas Shannon O'Brien, 352-90. Maryknoll: Orbis Books, 1996.

John Paul II. *Ecclesia De Eucharistia*. Washington, D.C.: United States Conference of Catholic Bishops, 2003.

John Paul II. *Familiaris Consortio: The Role of the Christian Family in the Modern World*. Anniversary Edition: With Commentary by John and Claire Grabowski ed. Boston: Pauline Books and Media, 2015.

Justin Martyr. *Dialogue with Trypho*. Translated by Thomas Falls. Washington, D.C.: The Catholic University Press, 2003.

Kandell, Jonathan. "Augusto Pinochet, Dictator Who Ruled by Terror in Chile, Dies at 91." *The New York Times*, December 11, 2006.

Kass, Leon. *The Hungry Soul: Eating and the Perfecting of Our Nature*. Chicago: The University of Chicago Press, 1999.

Kasza, John. *Understanding Sacramental Healing: Anointing and Viaticum*. Chicago: Hillenbrand Books, 2006.

Keating, Daniel. *Deification and Grace*. Naples: Sapientia Press, 2007.

Kelly, J.N.D. *Golden Mouth: The Story of John Chrysostom: Ascetic, Preacher, Bishop*. Grand Rapids: Baker Books, 1995.

Kennedy, Anthony. "Obergefell V. Hodges." edited by The United States Supreme Court. Washington, D.C., 2015.

Lane, Thomas. "The Jewish Temple Is Transfigured in Christ and the Temple Liturgies Are Transfigured in the Sacraments." *Antiphon* 19, no. 1 (2015): 14-28.

Laquer, Thomas. *The Work of the Dead: A Cultural History of Mortal Remains*. Princeton: Princeton University Press, 2015.

LaVerdiere, Eugene. *The Eucharist and the New Testament and the Early Church*. Collegeville: The Liturgical Press, 1996.

Lewis, C.S. "Introduction." In *St. Athanasius: On the Incarnation*, 3-10. Crestwood: St. Vladimir's Seminary Press, 1953.

Lewis, C.S. "Mere Christianity." In *The Complete C.S. Lewis Signature Classics*, 1-177. New York: HarperOne, 2002.

Long, Thomas. *Accompany Them with Singing: The Christian Funeral*. Louisville: Westminster John Knox Press, 2009.

Lubich, Chiara. *Essential Writings: Spirituality, Dialogue, Culture*. Hyde Park: New City Press, 2007.

Luther, Martin. "The Babylonian Captivity of the Church." In *Three Treatises*, 113-260. Philadelphia: Fortress Press, 1960.

Lynch, Thomas. *The Undertaking: Life Studies from the Dismal Trade*. New York: W. W. Norton & Company, 1997.

Martos, Joseph. *Doors to the Sacred: A Historical Introduction to Sacraments in the Catholic Church*. Vatican II Golden Anniversary ed. Liguori: Liguori Publications, 2014.

Mattison, William. *Introducing Moral Theology: True Happiness and the Virtues*. Grand Rapids: Brazos Press, 2008.

Meconi, David. "No Longer a Christian but Christ: Saint Augustine on Becoming Divine." In *Called to Be Children of God: The Catholic Theology of Human Deification*, 82-100. San Francisco: Ignatius Press, 2016.

Meconi, David and Carl Olson. "The Scriptural Roots of Christian Deification." In *Called to Be the Children of God: The Catholic Theology of Human Deification*, 17-29. San Francisco: Ignatius Press, 2016.

Merton, Thomas. *The Living Bread*. New York: Farrar, Straus and Cudahy, 1956.

Mich, Marvin. *Catholic Social Teaching and Movements*. Mystic: Twenty-Third Publications, 2000.

Miles, Sara. *Take This Bread: A Radical Conversion*. New York: Ballantine Books, 2007.

Mosser, Carl. "The Earliest Patristic Interpretations of Psalm 82, Jewish Antecedents, and the Origin of Christian Deification." *Journal of Theological Studies* 56, no. 1 (2005): 30-74.

Nouwen, Henri. *With Burning Hearts: A Meditation on the Eucharistic Life.* Maryknoll: Orbis Books, 2008.

O'Connor, Flannery. *The Habit of Being.* New York: Farrar, Straus, Giroux, 1979.

O'Connor, James. *The Hidden Manna: A Theology of the Eucharist.* San Francisco: Ignatius Press, 1988.

O'Malley, John. *Trent: What Happened at the Council.* Cambridge: The Belknap Press of Harvard University Press, 2013.

O'Malley, Timothy. *Real Presence: What Does It Mean and Why Does It Matter?* Notre Dame: Ave Maria Press, 2021.

Ortiz, Jared. "Deification in the Latin Fathers." In *Called to Be the Children of God: The Catholic Theology of Deification*, 59-81. San Francisco: Ignatius Press, 2016.

Ortiz, Jared. "Introduction." In *With All the Fullness of God: Deification in Christian Tradition*, 1-3. New York: Fortress Academic, 2021.

Ortiz, Jared. "The Whole Christ: Deification in the Catholic Tradition." In *With All the Fullness of God: Deification in Christian Tradition*, 7-28. New York: Fortress Academic, 2021.

Paredi, Angelo. *Saint Ambrose: His Life and Times.* Translated by M. Joseph Costelloe. Notre Dame: University of Notre Dame Press, 1964.

Paul VI. *Mysterium Fidei.* Boston: Pauline Books and Media, 1965.

Pitre, Brant. *Jesus and the Jewish Roots of the Eucharist.* New York: Doubleday, 2011.

Pius XII. *Mediator Dei.* New York: The America Press, 1947.

Plato. *The Republic.* Translated by Allan Bloom. New York: Basic Books: A Division of HarperCollins Publishers, 1968.

Plato. "Phaedo." In *The Last Days of Socrates*, 109-91. New York: Penguin, 1993.

Pontifical Council for Justice and Peace. *Compendium of the Social Doctrine of the Church.* Washington, D.C.: USCCB Publishing, 2007.

Ratzinger, Joseph Cardinal. "Eucharist, Communion, and Solidarity: Lecture Given at the Eucharistic Congress of the Archdiocese of Benevento, Italy." In *The Essential Pope Benedict XVI: His Central Writings and Speeches*, 69-84. New York: HarperOne, 2007.

Russell, Norman. *Fellow Workers with God: Orthodox Thinking on Theosis*. Crestwood: St. Vladimir's Seminary Press, 2009.

Sacred Congregation of Rites. *Eucharisticum Mysterium*: Vatican City, 1967.

Schmemann, Alexander. *The Eucharist: Sacrament of the Kingdom*. Translated by Paul Kachur. Crestwood: St Vladimir's Seminary Press, 1987.

Schönborn, Christoph. *The Source of Life: Exploring the Mystery of the Eucharist*. New York: Herder & Herder, 2007.

Scott, Margaret. *The Eucharist and Social Justice*. Mahwah: Paulist Press, 2009.

Sessa, Kristina. *Daily Life in Late Antiquity*. Cambridge: Cambridge University Press, 2018.

Sheen, Fulton. *The Mystical Body of Christ*. Notre Dame: Ave Maria Press, 2015.

Smith, Dennis. *From Symposium to Eucharist: The Banquet in the Early Christian World*. Minneapolis: Fortress Press, 2003.

Smith, Gregory. "Just One-Third of U.S. Catholics Agree with Their Church That Eucharist Is Body, Blood of Christ." (2019). https://www.pewresearch.org/facttank/2019/08/05/transubstantiation-eucharist-u-s-catholics/.

Stewart, Jon. *Kennedy Center Honors Tribute*. 2009.

Sullivan, Francis. *The Church We Believe In: One, Holy, Catholic, and Apostolic*. Mahwah: Paulist Press, 1988.

Thomas Aquinas. *Summa Theologica*. Translated by Fathers of the English Dominican Province. 5 vols. Westminster: Christian Classics, 1981.

United States Conference of Catholic Bishops. "Seven Themes of Catholic Social Teaching." Washington, D.C.: United States Conference of Catholic Bishops, 2015.

Valenzuela, Sebastián, Daniel Halpern, and James E. Katz. "Social Network Sites, Marriage Well-Being and Divorce: Survey and State-Level Evidence from the United States." *Computers in Human Behavior* 36 (2014): 94-101.

Van den Berg, Regina. "Like Another Christ: The Franciscan Theology of Deification." In *Called to Be Children of God: The Catholic Theology of Deification* 118-34. San Francisco: Ignatius Press, 2016.

Vatican II. "Apostolicam Actuositatem." In *Vatican Council II: The Basic Sixteen Documents*, edited by Austin Flannery, 403-42. Northport: Costello Publishing Company, 2007.

Vatican II. "Gaudium et Spes." In *Vatican Council II: The Basic Sixteen Documents*, edited by Austin Flannery, 163-282. Northport: Costello Publishing Company, 2007.

Vatican II. "Gravissimum Educationis." In *Vatican II: The Basic Sixteen Documents*, edited by Austin Flannery, 575-91. Northport: Costello Publishing Company, 2007.

Vatican II. "Lumen Gentium." In *Vatican Council II: The Basic Sixteen Documents*, edited by Austin Flannery, 1-95. Northport: Costello Publishing Company, 2007.

Vatican II. "Sacrosanctum Concilium." In *Vatican Council II: The Basic Sixteen Documents*, edited by Austin Flannery, 117-62. Northport: Costello Publishing Company, 2007.

Verhey, Allen. *The Christian Art of Dying: Learning from Jesus*. Grand Rapids: Wm. B. Eerdmans, 2011.

Wirix, Bert. "The Viaticum: From the Beginning until the Present Day." In *Bread of Heaven: Customs and Practices Surrounding Holy Communion*, 247-59. Kampen: Kok Pharos Publishing House, 1995.

Zeitz, Joshua. "*Born to Run* and the Decline of the American Dream: Bruce Springsteen's Breakout Album Embodied the Lost '70s— the Tense, Political, Working-Class Rejection of an Increasingly Unequal Society." *The Atlantic*, August 24, 2015.

Zwingli, Ulrich. "On the Lord's Supper." In *Zwingli and Bullinger*, edited by G.W. Bromiley, 176-238. Philadelphia: The Westminster Press, 1953.

Notes

1. Abigail Favale, *Into the Deep: An Unlikely Catholic Conversion* (Eugene: Cascade Books, 2018), 57-58; Timothy O'Malley, *Real Presence: What Does It Mean and Why Does It Matter?* (Notre Dame: Ave Maria Press, 2021), 4-5; Robert Barron, *Eucharist* (Maryknoll: Orbis Books, 2008), 95-97; James O'Connor, *The Hidden Manna: A Theology of the Eucharist* (San Francisco: Ignatius Press, 1988), 95.

2. Flannery O'Connor, *The Habit of Being* (New York: Farrar, Straus, Giroux, 1979), 125.

3. Catholic Church, *Catechism of the Catholic Church* (Vatican: Liberia Editrice Vaticana, 1994), 1374.

4. Gregory Smith, "Just One-Third of U.S. Catholics Agree with Their Church that Eucharist is Body, Blood of Christ," (2019). https://www.pewresearch.org/fact-tank/2019/08/05/transubstantiation-eucharist-u-s-catholics/ (accessed April 22, 2022).

5. Smith, "Just One-Third of U.S. Catholics Agree." For a discussion on some of the problematic language used in the study, see O'Malley, *Real Presence: What Does It Mean and Why Does It Matter?*, 1-2.

6. Robert Barron, "Bishop Barron on Catholics Misunderstanding the Eucharist," (2019). https://www.youtube.com/watch?v=0yTGlYCIvks (accessed August 6, 2022).

7. For example: Bernhard Blankenhorn, *Bread from Heaven: An Introduction to the Theology of the Eucharist* (Washington, D.C.: The Catholic University of America Press, 2021); Lawrence Feingold, *The Eucharist: Mystery of Presence, Sacrifice, and Communion* (Steubenville: Emmaus Academic 2018); O'Connor, *The Hidden Manna*; O'Malley, *Real Presence?*

8. Feingold, *The Eucharist*, 40.

9. For discussions of the Jewish Temple, see Alfred Edersheim, *The Temple: Its Ministry and Services*, Updated ed. (Peabody: Hendrickson, 1994); Joshua Berman, *The Temple: Its Symbolism and Meaning Then and Now* (Eugene: Wipf and Stock, 2010).

10. For a more detailed description of the Bread of the Face, see Edersheim, *The Temple*, 140-45; Berman, *The Temple*, 136-38; Feingold, *The Eucharist*, 63-66; Brant Pitre, *Jesus and the Jewish Roots of the Eucharist* (New York: Doubleday, 2011), 116-46.

11. Edersheim, *The Temple*, 143-44.

12. Psalm 69:10 reads "...zeal for your house has consumed me."

13. Anonymous, "Didache," in *Early Christian Fathers* (New York: Touchstone, 1996), 161-79; Feingold, *The Eucharist*, 129-32; O'Connor, *The Hidden Manna Eucharist*, 5-9; Mike Aquilina, *The Mass of the Early Christians*, Second ed. (Huntington: Our Sunday Visitor, 2007), 63-68.

14. Anonymous, "Didache," 175.

15. Anonymous, "Didache," 175-76.

16. Anonymous, "Didache," 176.

17. Ignatius of Antioch, "Epistles," in *Early Christian Fathers* (New York: Touchstone, 1996), 103.

18. Ignatius of Antioch, "Epistles,"105.

19. Ignatius of Antioch, "Epistles,"104.

20. Ignatius of Antioch, "Epistles,"105.

21. Ignatius of Antioch, "Epistles,"115.

22. Ignatius of Antioch, "Epistles,"113.

23. Ignatius of Antioch, "Epistles,"114.

24. Barron, *Eucharist*, 113.

25. Feingold, *The Eucharist*, 260.

26. Feingold, *The Eucharist*, 260.

27. John O'Malley, *Trent: What Happened at the Council* (Cambridge: The Belknap Press of Harvard University Press, 2013), 14-15.

28. Martin Luther, "The Babylonian Captivity of the Church," in *Three Treatises* (Philadelphia: Fortress Press, 1960), 144-45.

29. Ulrich Zwingli, "On the Lord's Supper," in *Zwingli and Bullinger*, ed. G.W. Bromiley (Philadelphia: The Westminster Press, 1953), 188.

30. John Calvin, *Institutes of the Christian Religion*, trans., Ford Lewis Battles (Philadelphia: The Westminster Press, 1960), 1362.

31. Council of Trent, *The Canons and Decrees of the Council of Trent*, trans., H.J. Schroeder (Rockford: Tan Books and Publishers, 1978), 73.

32. Council of Trent, *The Canons and Decrees*, 75.

33. Alexander Schmemann, *The Eucharist: Sacrament of the Kingdom*, trans., Paul Kachur (Crestwood: St Vladimir's Seminary Press, 1987), 124.

34. Schmemann, *The Eucharist: Sacrament of the Kingdom*, 124.

35. Kevin Irwin, *Models of the Eucharist* (Mahwah: Paulist Press, 2005), 125.

36. Irwin, *Models of the Eucharist*, 102.

37. Irwin, *Models of the Eucharist*, 102.

38. Irwin, *Models of the Eucharist*, 125-26.

39. John Paul II, *Ecclesia de Eucharistia* (Washington, D.C.: United States Conference of Catholic Bishops, 2003), 5.

40. John Paul II, *Ecclesia de Eucharistia*, 11.

41. Louis Bouyer, *Eucharist: Theology and Spirituality of the Eucharistic Prayer*, trans., Charles Quinn (Notre Dame: University of Notre Dame Press, 1968), 103-4.

42. Merton, *The Living Bread*, 27.

43. Christoph Schönborn, *The Source of Life: Exploring the Mystery of the Eucharist* (New York: Herder & Herder, 2007), 57.

44. For an excellent biography of St. Monica, see: Gillian Clark, *Monica: An Ordinary Saint* (Oxford: Oxford University Press, 2015).

45. Clark, *Monica: An Ordinary Saint*, 17.

46. Augustine, *Confessions*, trans., Henry Chadwick (Oxford: Oxford World Classics, 1998), 9.11.27.

47. Augustine, *Confessions*, 9.11.28.

48. John Cavadini, "Eucharistic Exegesis in Augustine's *Confessions*," *Augustinian Studies* 41:1 (2010): 88.

49. Feingold, *The Eucharist*, 327; Berman, *The Temple* 115.

50. Scott Hahn, *The Fourth Cup*, 43-44.

51. Berman, *The Temple*, 116.

52. Berman, *The Temple*, 48-52.

53. Barron, *Eucharist*, 66-67; Scott Hahn, *Catholic Bible Dictionary* (New York: Doubleday, 2009), 795.

54. Scott Hahn, *The Lamb's Supper: The Mass as Heaven on Earth* (New York: Doubleday, 1999), 19; James O'Connor, *The Hidden Manna*, 300-01.

55. Merton, *The Living Bread*, 22.

56. Merton, *The Living Bread*, 22-23.

57. Hahn, *The Fourth Cup*, 36.

58. Feingold, *The Eucharist*, 406.

59. Thomas Lane, "The Jewish Temple is Transfigured in Christ and the Temple Liturgies are Transfigured in the Sacraments," *Antiphon* 19, no. 1 (2015): 14-28.

60. The Rabbis categorized seventy-three possible blemishes. Edersheim, *The Temple*, 78.

61. For a more detailed description of these five offerings, see: Edersheim, *The Temple*, 90-104; Hahn, *Catholic Bible Dictionary*, 792-94.

62. Berman, *The Temple*, 118.

63. Berman, *The Temple*, 139.

64. Augustine, *Questions on the Heptateuch*, 2.73, as quoted in Benedict XVI, *Verbum Domini* (Washington, D.C.: The United States Conference of Catholic Bishops, 2010), 41.

65. Benedict XVI, *Verbum Domini*, 40.

66. As quoted in Pitre, *Jesus and the Jewish Roots of the Eucharist*, 63-64.

67. Justin Martyr, *Dialogue with Trypho*. Translated by Thomas Falls (Washington, D.C.: The Catholic University Press, 2003), 40.

68. Merton, *The Living Bread*, 24.

69. For a description of how the Last Supper extended into the crucifixion, see Pitre, *Jesus and the Jewish Roots of the Eucharist*, 145-70; Hahn, *The Fourth Cup*, 17-182.

70. For a review of the similarities and differences between a typical Passover meal and the Last Supper, see: Pitre, *Jesus and the Jewish Roots of the Eucharist*, 68-76.

71. The NABRE translation says "His life as a reparation [guilt] offering." Here I have used the NIV translation (and others) "his life an offering for sin," which helps clarify the connection.

72. In Mark and Matthew, Jesus first took the bread, then the cup. In Luke, he took the cup first, then took the bread. John does not have an institution narrative.

73. The NABRE translation says "surrendered himself to death," but other translations such as NIV, English Standard, King James, New King James, New American Standard, and others render the phrase "poured out."

74. John Chrysostom, *Homilies on the Epistle to the Hebrews*, 17.3, 6. As quoted in Feingold, *The Eucharist* 340. For an excellent biography of Chrysostom, see J.N.D. Kelly, *Golden Mouth: The Story of John Chrysostom: Ascetic, Preacher, Bishop* (Grand Rapids: Baker Books, 1995).

75. Pius XII called it a "commemorative representation." See Pius XII, *Mediator Dei* (New York: The America Press, 1947), 70.

76. Barron, *Eucharist*, 88.

77. John Paul II, *Ecclesia de Eucharistia*, 11.

78. Council of Trent, *The Canons and Decrees of the Council of Trent*, 144.

79. Catholic Church, *Catechism of the Catholic Church*, 1367.

80. Berman, *The Temple*, 48-52.

81. Cyprian, "The Epistles of Cyprian," in *Ante-Nicene Fathers: Hippolytus, Cyprian, Caius, Novatian, Appendix* (Peabody: Hendrickson Publishers, 2004), 62.13. I have modified the translation slightly to render the English more modern.

82. Augustine, *Confessions*, 7.10.16.

83. Benedict XVI, *Sacramentum Caritatis*, 71.

84. Norman Russell, *Fellow Workers with God: Orthodox Thinking on Theosis* (Crestwood: St. Vladimir's Seminary Press, 2009), 22.

85. Jared Ortiz, "The Whole Christ: Deification in the Catholic Tradition," in *With All the Fullness of God: Deification in Christian Tradition* (New York: Fortress Academic, 2021), 8.

86. *Ecclesiastical Hierarchy* 1.3, As quoted in Russell, *Fellow Workers with God: Orthodox Thinking on Theosis*, 21-2.

87. Daniel Keating has said that deification is "a term that describes specifically our supernatural participation in God. Conformed into the likeness of the Son through the Spirit, we become adopted sons and daughters of the Father, and share in the divine life of God. Supernatural participation is not less real than our participation in being; rather, it is of a different order, and indeed, a more elevated and privileged participation in God. It is a personal participation in God—through grace we enter into the personal communion of love of the Father, Son, and Holy Spirit." Norman Russell has said that deification "is our restoration as persons to integrity and wholeness by participation in Christ through the Holy Spirit, in a process which is initiated in this world through our life of ecclesial communion and moral striving and finds ultimate fulfillment in our union with the Father—all within the broad context of the divine economy." Daniel Keating, *Deification and Grace* (Naples: Sapientia Press, 2007), 100; Russell, *Fellow Workers with God: Orthodox Thinking on Theosis*, 21.

88. Ortiz, "The Whole Christ: Deification in the Catholic Tradition," 8.

89. Augustine's *Expositions on the Psalms*, 49.2 as quoted in Keating, *Deification and Grace*, 93.

90. Keating, *Deification and Grace*, 97.

91. In his encyclical *Evangelium Vitae*, John Paul II explained that "God proclaims that he is absolute Lord of the life of man, who is formed in his image and likeness (Gn 1:26-28). Human life is thus given a sacred and inviolable character, which reflects the inviolability of the Creator

himself. Precisely for this reason God will severely judge every violation of the commandment 'You shall not kill,' the commandment which is at the basis of all life together in society." Because of this inherent sacredness that cannot be lost, increased, or decreased, the Catholic Church stands staunchly against all violations of the human person: murder, genocide, abortion, euthanasia, willful self-destruction, subhuman living conditions, arbitrary imprisonment, deportation, slavery, prostitution, disgraceful working conditions, and whenever people are treated as instruments use." John Paul II, *Evangelium vitae*, 53; Vatican II, "Gaudium et Spes," 27.

92. David Meconi and Carl Olson, "The Scriptural Roots of Christian Deification," in *Called to Be the Children of God: The Catholic Theology of Human Deification* (San Francisco: Ignatius Press, 2016), 18-22.

93. Carl Mosser, "The Earliest Patristic Interpretations of Psalm 82, Jewish Antecedents, and the Origin of Christian Deification," *Journal of Theological Studies* 56, no. 1 (2005): 35-41.

94. Russell, *Fellow Workers with God*, 55-64.

95. Russell, *Fellow Workers with God*, 60.

96. Keating, *Deification and Grace*, 16-17; Meconi and Olson, "The Scriptural Roots of Christian Deification," 30-36; Jared Ortiz, "Introduction," in *With All the Fullness of God: Deification in Christian Tradition* (New York: Fortress Academic, 2021), 1.

97. As quoted in Meconi and Olson, "The Scriptural Roots of Christian Deification," 31.

98. Russell, *Fellow Workers with God*, 65-71; Keating, *Deification and Grace*, 33-37; Meconi and Olson, "The Scriptural Roots of Christian Deification," 36-37.

99. Catholic Church, *Catechism of the Catholic Church*, 1.

100. Athanasius, *On the Incarnation*, trans., A Religious of C.S.M.V. (Crestwood: St. Vladimir's Press, 1953), 54.

101. David Meconi, "No Longer a Christian but Christ: Saint Augustine on Becoming Divine," in *Called to Be Children of God: The Catholic Theology of Human Deification* (San Francisco: Ignatius Press, 2016), 82-94. Earlier, we saw that the rabbinic tradition as well as the Christian tradition starting with Justin Martyr claimed that Adam and Eve were gods before the fall. Here, we see Augustine claim that they were not gods before the fall. This may seem to be contradictory. Mosser points out that, for Justin, to be gods before the fall meant that Adam and Eve were immortal and impassible. For Augustine, according to Meconi, they were not gods before the fall in the sense that they were not intended by God to be "merely" humans, but that God intended them to be "more than human."

To make this point, Meconi notes that, in his *The Trinity*, Augustine says that "divinity cannot be seen by human sight in any way whatever; it is seen by a power of sight which makes those who already see with it not human but superhuman (*ultra homines*)" (1.6.11). Therefore, there does not seem to be a contradiction between Justin claiming that Adam and Eve were gods before the fall, and Augustine claiming that they were not gods before the fall. Mosser, "The Earliest Patristic Interpretations of Psalm 82, Jewish Antecedents, and the Origin of Christian Deification," 38-39; Meconi, "No Longer a Christian but Christ: Saint Augustine on Becoming Divine," 86; Augustine, *The Trinity*, trans., Edmund Hill (Hyde Park: New City Press, 1991), 1.6.11.

102. Augustine, *Homilies on the Gospel of John*, 21.8 as quoted in Meconi, "No Longer a Christian But Christ: Saint Augustine on Becoming Divine," 94-5.

103. David Fagerberg, "Liturgy and Divinization," in *Called to Be Children of God: The Catholic Theology of Human Deification* (San Francisco: Ignatius Press, 2016), 274.

104. Ortiz, "Making Worshipers into Gods: Deification in the Latin Liturgy," 23; Keating, *Deification and Grace*, 44. See also: Regina Van den Berg, "Like Another Christ: The Franciscan Theology of Deification," in *Called to Be Children of God: The Catholic Theology of Deification* (San Francisco: Ignatius Press, 2016), 122.

105. Cyril of Jerusalem, "Catechetical Lectures," in *Nicene and Post-Nicene Fathers: Cyril of Jerusalem, Gregory Nazianzen* (Peabody: Hendrickson Publishers, 2004), 22.3. I have updated the translation to modern English.

106. Augustine, *Homilies on the Gospel of John*, 27.6 as quoted in Meconi, "No Longer a Christian but Christ: Saint Augustine on Becoming Divine," 96.

107. Chiara Lubich, *Essential Writings: Spirituality, Dialogue, Culture* (Hyde Park: New City Press, 2007), 129.

108. Merton, *The Living Bread*, 119.

109. Feingold, *The Eucharist*, 506; Eugene LaVerdiere, *The Eucharist and the New Testament and the Early Church* (Collegeville: The Liturgical Press, 1996), 66.

110. Catholic Church, *Catechism of the Catholic Church*, 1394; Feingold, *The Eucharist]*, 506 and 526.

111. Catholic Church, *Catechism of the Catholic Church*, 1862.

112. Catholic Church, *Catechism of the Catholic Church*, 1395.

113. Catholic Church, *Catechism of the Catholic Church*, 1857.

114. Catholic Church, *Catechism of the Catholic Church*, 1856.

115. Catholic Church, *Catechism of the Catholic Church*, 1415.

116. Catholic Church, *Catechism of the Catholic Church*, 1393; Feingold, *The Eucharist*, 526.

117. Catholic Church, *Catechism of the Catholic Church*, 1395; Feingold, *The Eucharist*, 506-08.

118. Benedict XVI, *Sacramentum Caritatis*, 82.

119. Merton, *The Living Bread*, 115 and 122; Paul VI, *Mysterium Fidei* (Boston: Pauline Books and Media, 1965), 67.

120. William Mattison, *Introducing Moral Theology: True Happiness and the Virtues* (Grand Rapids: Brazos Press, 2008), 57-74.

121. Mattison, *Introducing Moral Theology*, 213-30, 251-72, 290-310.

122. See also: Lv 11:44.

123. Vatican II, "Lumen Gentium," in *Vatican Council II: The Basic Sixteen Documents*, ed. Austin Flannery (Northport: Costello Publishing Company, 2007), 39-42.

124. Vatican II, "Sacrosanctum Concilium," in *Vatican Council II: The Basic Sixteen Documents*, ed. Austin Flannery (Northport: Costello Publishing Company, 2007), 10.

125. Cyril of Jerusalem, "Catechetical Lectures," 22.5; Pius XII, *Mediator Dei*, 17; Merton, *The Living Bread*, 121; Benedict XVI, *Sacramentum Caritatis*, 94; Ortiz, "Deification in the Latin Fathers," 66.

126. Cyril of Alexandria, "Commentary on Luke, Sermon 127," https://www.tertullian.org/fathers/cyril_on_luke_12_sermons_124_134.htm#SERMON%20CXXVII (accessed May 28th, 2021).

127. Cyril of Alexandria, "Commentary on Luke, Sermon 127."

128. It is often the case with the Bible that biblical passages have a deeper meaning. For example, at the beginning of the story of the Canaanite woman, we are told that Jesus "went from that place [Gennesaret] and withdrew to the region of Tyre and Sidon" (Mt 15:21). On the surface level, this seems to say that Jesus went from point A to point B. Every first-century Jew reading this story would know that the region of Tyre and Sidon is a Gentile region. Spiritually, then, the Gospel of Matthew is telling us that Jesus was incarnate for Jews and Gentiles.

129. Augustine, *Sermons (230-272B), The Works of Saint Augustine: A Translation for the 21st Century*, vol. III/7 (Hyde Park: New City Press, 1993), 235.2.

130. Augustine, *Sermons (230-272B)*, 235.3.

131. We see a similar example of this in the story of Jesus walking on the water. After Peter started to walk on the water, Peter turned his attention away from Jesus to the wind, became frightened, and began to sink (Mt 14: 28-31).

132. Augustine, *Sermons (230-272B)*, 236.2.

133. Augustine, *Letters: 100-155*, ed. Boniface Ramsey, trans., Boniface Ramsey, *The Works of Saint Augustine: A Translation for the 21st Century* (Hyde Park: New City Press, 2003), 149.32.

134. While traveling at night in the twenty-first century is common and easy because of electric lights, returning to Jerusalem at night for these disciples presumably was difficult and dangerous. Their renewed faith prevented any fear.

135. Cyril of Alexandria, *Commentary of the Gospel of John*, 11.11.

136. Joseph Ratzinger, "Eucharist, Communion, and Solidarity: Lecture Given at the Eucharistic Congress of the Archdiocese of Benevento, Italy." In *The Essential Pope Benedict XVI: His Central Writings and Speeches* (New York: HarperOne, 2007), 83.

137. Leon Kass, *The Hungry Soul: Eating and the Perfecting of Our Nature* (Chicago: The University of Chicago Press, 1999), 134-35.

138. Kass, *The Hungry Soul*, 126.

139. Kass, *The Hungry Soul*, 146.

140. One exception, of course, is intimacy through the sexual act. But the sexual act is restricted to married couples, while sharing a meal can be done between any two people.

141. From the *Quaestiones Convivales* 612D; 660B as quoted in Dennis Smith, *From Symposium to Eucharist: The Banquet in the Early Christian World* (Minneapolis: Fortress Press, 2003), 55.

142. The Christian understanding of friendship is rooted in the Aristotelian understanding of friendship. See Aristotle. "Nicomachean Ethics." In *Introduction to Aristotle*, edited by Richard McKeon (New York: The Modern Library, 1947), 9.9.

143. John Cassian, *The Conferences*. Translated by Boniface Ramsey. Vol. 57. Ancient Christian Writers (New York: The Newman Press, 1997), 16.3.4. In the text, Abba Joseph spoke these words. Scholars have long debated if the quotations from desert abbas in Cassian's writings are word-for-word quotations, summaries, or avatars for Cassian himself.

144. Gregory Boyle, *Tattoos on the Heart: The Power of Boundless Compassion* (New York: Free Press, 2010), 188.

145. Boyle, *Tattoos on the Heart,* 187.

146. Boyle, *Tattoos on the Heart,* 140-142.

147. Smith, *From Symposium to Eucharist,* 14-18.

148. Cavanaugh, *Theopolitical Imagination,* 13.

149. Catholic Church, *Catechism of the Catholic Church,* 790 and 1398.

150. Irwin, *Models of the Eucharist,* 181.

151. Francis Sullivan, *The Church We Believe In: One, Holy, Catholic, and Apostolic* (Mahwah: Paulist Press, 1988), 34-65.

152. Cyprian, "On the Unity of the Church." In *Ante-Nicene Fathers: Hippolytus, Cyprian, Caius, Novatian, Appendix* (Peabody: Hendrickson Publishers, 2004), 5.

153. Cyprian, "On the Unity of the Church," 6.

154. Cantalamessa, *The Eucharist: Our Sanctification,* 16.

155. John Paul II, *Ecclesia de Eucharistia,* 21.

156. John Paul II, *Ecclesia de Eucharistia,* 23.

157. Catholic Church, *Catechism of the Catholic Church,* 1396. I added a comma after the word "it" for clarity.

158. Harrington, *The Church According to the New Testament,* 83-85.

159. See also Acts 11:27-30; Rom 15:25-27; 1 Cor 16:1-4; 2 Cor 8-9.

160. Harrington, *The Church According to the New Testament,* 92.

161. Harrington, *The Church According to the New Testament* 162-65.

162. Ignatius, "Epistles," 89.

163. Sullivan, *The Church We Believe In,* 47-48.

164. William Cavanaugh, *Torture and Eucharist: Theology, Politics, and the Body of Christ* (Malden: Blackwell Publishing, 1998), 12.

165. Cavanaugh, *Torture and Eucharist,* 205.

166. Cavanaugh, *Torture and Eucharist,* 25-27. In 1977, the CNI (*Central Nacional de Informationes*) continued the terror of the DINA after the DINA had been disbanded.

167. Cavanaugh, *Torture and Eucharist,* 26-27.

168. Cavanaugh, *Torture and Eucharist,* 66.

169. Jonathan Kandell, "Augusto Pinochet, Dictator Who Ruled by Terror in Chile, Dies at 91." *The New York Times,* December 11th, 2006.

170. Cavanaugh, *Torture and Eucharist,* 28-31.

171. Cavanaugh, *Torture and Eucharist,* 22.

172. Cavanaugh, *Torture and Eucharist,* 34.

173. Cavanaugh, *Torture and Eucharist,* 253-64.

174. Cavanaugh, *Torture and Eucharist,* 253-62.

175. Cavanaugh, *Torture and Eucharist,* 264-66.

176. Cavanaugh, *Torture and Eucharist,* 267.

177. Cavanaugh, *Torture and Eucharist,* 267.

178. Cavanaugh, *Torture and Eucharist,* 267.

179. Cavanaugh, *Torture and Eucharist,* 273.

180. Cavanaugh, *Torture and Eucharist,* 275.

181. Cavanaugh, *Torture and Eucharist,* 276.

182. Marvin Mich, *Catholic Social Teaching and Movements* (Mystic: Twenty-Third Publications, 2000), 1.

183. Feingold, *The Eucharist,* 503.

184. The United States Conference of Catholic Bishops, "Seven Themes of Catholic Social Teaching." Washington, D.C.: United States Conference of Catholic Bishops, 2015.

185. Augustine, *The Trinity,* trans., Edmund Hill (Hyde Park: New City Press, 1991), 12.4.25.

186. Plato, *The Republic,* trans., Allan Bloom (New York: Basic Books: A Division of HarperCollins Publishers, 1968), 369a.

187. Thomas Aquinas, *Summa Theologica,* trans., Fathers of the English Dominican Province, 5 vols. (Westminster: Christian Classics, 1981), IIa-IIae q. 58 a. 1.

188. Vatican II, "Lumen Gentium," 5.39-42.

189. Vatican II, "Lumen Gentium," 5.40.

190. Vatican II, "Gaudium et Spes," in *Vatican Council II: The Basic Sixteen Documents,* ed. Austin Flannery (Northport: 2007), Intro.9.

191. Vatican II, "Gaudium et Spes," Introduction.

192. "Communities of Salt and Light: Reflections on the Social Mission of the Parish," https://www.usccb.org/resources/communities-salt-and-light-reflections-social-mission-parish.

193. The United States Conference of Catholic Bishops, "Seven Themes of Catholic Social Teaching."

194. Pontifical Council for Justice and Peace, *Compendium of the Social Doctrine of the Church* (Washington, D.C.: USCCB Publishing, 2007), 107.

195. The inherent sacredness of the human person is the ground for the Christian claim of the radical equality of all human beings regardless of gender, nationality, race, social class, or culture. Pontifical Council for Justice and Peace, *Compendium*, 144.

196. The United States Conference of Catholic Bishops, "Seven Themes of Catholic Social Teaching."

197. John Paul II, *Familiaris Consortio* (Boston: Pauline Books, 1981), 42; Vatican II, "Apostolicam Actuositatem," in *Vatican Council II: The Basic Sixteen Documents*, ed. Austin Flannery (Northport: Costello Publishing Company, 2007), 11.

198. John Paul II, *Familiaris Consortio*, 14, 36, 44.

199. Vatican II, "Gravissimum Educationis," in *Vatican II: The Basic Sixteen Documents*, ed. Austin Flannery (Northport: Costello Publishing Company, 2007), 1.

200. Pontifical Council for Justice and Peace, *Compendium*, 210-12.

201. Pontifical Council for Justice and Peace, *Compendium*, 212, 470.

202. Pontifical Council for Justice and Peace, *Compendium*, 212.

203. Pontifical Council for Justice and Peace, *Compendium*, 470.

204. John Paul II, *Familiaris Consortio*, 17; Pontifical Council for Justice and Peace, *Compendium*, 211.

205. John Paul II, *Familiaris Consortio*, 17.

206. John Paul II, *Familiaris Consortio*, 17-18.

207. John Paul II, *Familiaris Consortio*, 17, 28.

208. John Paul II, *Familiaris Consortio*, 17, 43.

209. John Paul II, *Familiaris Consortio*, 17, 49.

210. John Paul II, *Familiaris Consortio*, 1.

211. John Paul II, *Familiaris Consortio*, 6-7.

212. John Paul II, *Familiaris Consortio*, 3.

213. John Paul II, *Familiaris Consortio*, 7.

214. Sebastián Valenzuela, Daniel Halpern, and James E. Katz, "Social Network Sites, Marriage Well-Being and Divorce: Survey and State-Level Evidence from the United States," *Computers in Human Behavior* 36 (2014): 94-101.

215. Justice Anthony Kennedy summarized the definition of marriage according to our dominant American culture: marriage "has promised nobility and

dignity to all persons, without regard to their station in life. Marriage is sacred to those who live by their religions and offers unique fulfillment to those who find meaning in the secular realm. Its dynamic allows two people to find a life that could not be found alone, for a marriage becomes greater than just the two persons. Rising from the most basic human needs, marriage is essential to our most profound hopes and aspirations." Anthony Kennedy, *Obergefell v. Hodges*, ed. The United States Supreme Court (Washington, D.C.: 2015), IIA.

216. The United States Conference of Catholic Bishops, "Seven Themes."

217. John Paul II, *Evangelium Vitae* (Boston: Pauline Books and Media, 1995), 12.

218. John Paul II, *Evangelium Vitae*, 23.

219. John Paul II, *Evangelium Vitae*, 99.

220. John Paul II, *Evangelium Vitae*, 19.

221. John Paul II, *Evangelium Vitae*, 20.

222. John Paul II, *Evangelium Vitae*, 63.

223. John Paul II, *Evangelium Vitae*, 4, 89.

224. The United States Conference of Catholic Bishops, "Seven Themes."

225. Dorothy Day, *Loaves and Fishes: The Inspiring Story of the Catholic Worker Movement* (Maryknoll: Orbis Books, 1997), 104.

226. See Dorothy Day, *The Long Loneliness: The Autobiography of the Legendary Catholic Social Activist* (New York: HarperOne, 1997). See also Kate Hennessy, *Dorothy Day: The World Will Be Saved by Beauty* (New York: Scribner, 2017).

227. Day, *Loaves and Fishes*, 34.

228. Day, *Loaves and Fishes*, 7.

229. Day, *Loaves and Fishes*, 17-18.

230. Day, *Loaves and Fishes*, 39-41.

231. Day, *Loaves and Fishes*, 23.

232. Day, *Loaves and Fishes*, 156-58.

233. Day, *Loaves and Fishes*, 29.

234. Day, *Loaves and Fishes*, 42-43.

235. Day, *Loaves and Fishes*, 44.

236. Day, *Loaves and Fishes*, 23.

237. Day, *Loaves and Fishes*, 45.

238. Day, *Loaves and Fishes*, 55.

239. The United States Conference of Catholic Bishops, "Seven Themes."

240. John Paul II, *Laborem Exercens*, in *Catholic Social Thought: The Documentary Heritage*, ed. Obrien, David and Thomas Shannon (Maryknoll: Orbis Books, 1996), 4.

241. John Paul II, *Laborem Exercens*, 27.

242. John Paul II, *Laborem Exercens*, 6.

243. John Paul II, *Laborem Exercens*, 9.

244. The United States Conference of Catholic Bishops, "Seven Themes."

245. Francis, *Fratelli Tutti* (Huntington: Our Sunday Visitor, 2020), 43.

246. Francis, *Fratelli Tutti*, 43.

247. Francis, *Fratelli Tutti*, 43.

248. Francis, *Fratelli Tutti*, 43.

249. Francis, *Fratelli Tutti*, 44-46.

250. Plato, *The Republic*, 2:359a-2:360d.

251. Francis, *Fratelli Tutti*, 44.

252. Francis, *Fratelli Tutti*, 45.

253. Francis, *Fratelli Tutti*, 46.

254. Francis, *Fratelli Tutti*, 46-50.

255. Francis, *Fratelli Tutti*, 49-50.

256. Francis, *Fratelli Tutti*, 47.

257. Francis, *Fratelli Tutti*, 47.

258. Francis, *Fratelli Tutti*, 115.

259. Francis, *Fratelli Tutti*, 116.

260. Francis, *Fratelli Tutti*, 115.

261. The United States Conference of Catholic Bishops, "Seven Themes."

262. Francis, *Laudato Si'*, 21.

263. Francis, *Laudato Si'*, 22.

264. Francis, "Pope in Bolivia: No One Needs to be Discarded," *America Magazine* https://www.americamagazine.org/issue/pope-bolivia-no-one-needs-be-discarded (accessed October 10th, 2021).

265. Francis, *Laudato Si'*, 28, 30.

266. Francis, *Laudato Si'*, 28.

267. Francis, *Laudato Si'*, 30.

268. Francis, *Laudato Si'*, 29.

269. Francis, *Laudato Si'*, 30.

270. Francis, *Laudato Si'*, 31.

271. Francis, *Laudato Si'*, 204.

272. Francis, *Laudato Si'*, 203-08.

273. Francis, *Laudato Si'*, 231.

274. Francis, *Laudato Si'*, 231.

275. Francis, *Laudato Si'*, 228-31.

276. Lewis, *Mere Christianity*, 109.

277. John Paul II, *Dominicae Cenae*, 6.

278. John Paul II, *Dominicae Cenae*, 5.

279. John Paul II, *Dominicae Cenae*, 5.

280. Catholic Church, *Catechism of the Catholic Church*, 1397; Scott, *The Eucharist and Social Justice*, 6; Benedict XVI *Sacramentum Caritatis*, 90.

281. Benedict XVI, *Caritas in Veritate*, 2.

282. Benedict XVI, *Caritas in Veritate*, 1.

283. Benedict XVI *Sacramentum Caritatis*, 76.

284. Smith, *From Symposium to Eucharist: The Banquet in the Early Christian World*, 14-18.

285. Glancy, Jennifer. *Slavery in Early Christianity* (Minneapolis: Fortress Press, 2006), 45.

286. John Paul II, *Ecclesia De Eucharistia*, 20.

287. Nouwen, *With Burning Hearts*, 103.

288. It should be noted that Miles is a convert to the Episcopalian tradition, not Catholicism. Although the Catholic Church does not recognize the Episcopalian celebration of the Eucharist as valid, it cannot be denied that her experience was radically transformative. Would that all Catholics be as transformed by the Eucharist as she is.

289. Sara Miles, *Take this Bread: A Radical Conversion* (New York: Ballantine Books, 2007), xii.

290. Miles, *Take this Bread,* 57.

291. Miles, *Take this Bread,* xiii.

292. Miles, *Take this Bread,* 57.

293. Miles, *Take this Bread,* 58.

294. Miles, *Take this Bread,* 58.

295. Miles, *Take this Bread,* 59.

296. Miles, *Take this Bread,* 59.

297. Miles, *Take this Bread,* 60.

298. Miles, *Take this Bread,* 61.

299. Miles, *Take this Bread,* 97.

300. Miles, *Take this Bread,* 93.

301. Miles, *Take this Bread,* 113.

302. Miles, *Take this Bread,* 104.

303. Miles, *Take this Bread,* 129.

304. Feingold, *The Eucharist,* 573.

305. Bert Wirix, "The Viaticum: From the Beginning Until the Present Day," in *Bread of Heaven: Customs and Practices Surrounding Holy Communion* (Kampen: Kok Pharos Publishing House, 1995), 247.

306. Sacred Congregation of Rites, *Eucharisticum Mysterium* (Vatican City, 1967), 39; Wirix, "The Viaticum," 247-48.

307. David Grumett, *Material Eucharist* (Oxford: Oxford University Press, 2016), 193.

308. Feingold, *The Eucharist,* 573.

309. John Kasza, *Understanding Sacramental Healing: Anointing and Viaticum* (Chicago: Hillenbrand Books, 2006), 197-98.

310. Wirix, "The Viaticum," 257.

311. Wirix, "The Viaticum," 258.

312. Cicero's *Tusculan Disputations* as quoted in Thomas Laquer, *The Work of the Dead: A Cultural History of Mortal Remains* (Princeton: Princeton University Press, 2015), 1.

313. Plato, "Phaedo," in *The Last Days of Socrates* (New York: Penguin, 1993), 82e.

314. Plato, "Phaedo," 66b-67b.

315. Plato, "Phaedo," 65c.

316. Plato, "Phaedo," 66e.

317. Thomas Lynch, *The Undertaking: Life Studies from the Dismal Trade* (New York: W. W. Norton & Company, 1997), 20.

318. Meconi, "No Longer a Christian but Christ," 82-94.

319. See also 1 Jn 4:2.

320. Plato, "Phaedo," 64c.

321. Thomas Long, *Accompany Them with Singing: The Christian Funeral* (Louisville: Westminster John Knox Press, 2009), 3-4; Allen Verhey, *The Christian Art of Dying: Learning From Jesus* (Grand Rapids: Wm. B. Eerdmans, 2011), 11-13.

322. Verhey, *The Christian Art of Dying*, 11-23.

323. Verhey, *The Christian Art of Dying*, 13.

324. Verhey, *The Christian Art of Dying*, 14.

325. Verhey, *The Christian Art of Dying*, 14.

326. Verhey, *The Christian Art of Dying*, 15-17.

327. L.S. Dugdale, *The Lost Art of Dying: Reviving Forgotten Wisdom* (New York: HarperOne, 2020), 96.

328. Dugdale, *The Lost Art of Dying*, 96-111.

329. Dugdale, *The Lost Art of Dying*, 99.

330. Dugdale, *The Lost Art of Dying*, 96-99.

331. Dugdale, *The Lost Art of Dying*, 99.

332. Angelo Paredi, *Saint Ambrose: His Life and Times*, trans., M. Joseph Costelloe (Notre Dame: University of Notre Dame Press, 1964), 167-72.

333. Ambrose, "On the Death of Satyrus," in *Nicene and Post-Nicene Fathers: Ambrose: Select Works and Letters* (Peabody: Hendrickson Publishers, 2004), 2.39.

334. Ambrose, "On the Death of Satyrus," 2.40.

335. Ambrose, "On the Death of Satyrus," 2.47.

336. Ambrose, "On the Death of Satyrus," 2.3.

337. Ambrose, "On the Death of Satyrus," 2.49.

338. Ambrose, "On the Death of Satyrus," 2.18.

339. Ambrose, "On the Death of Satyrus," 2.37.

340. Ambrose, "On the Death of Satyrus," 2.46.

341. Christopher Hitchens, "Hitchens Takes on Mother Teresa," *Newsweek* Sept. 10, 2007 http://bit.ly/vGzuqh #HitchReads.

342. Christopher Hitchens, "Is There an Afterlife? - Christopher Hitchens, Sam Harris, David Wolpe, Bradley Artson Shavit" https://www.youtube.com/watch?v=UjKJ92b9Y04 (accessed February 5th, 2022).

343. Stephen Hawking, "Stephen Hawking: 'There is No Heaven; It's a Fairy Story,'" in *The Guardian*, ed. Ian Sample (2011).

344. Stephen Hawking, "Stephen Hawking: 'There is No Heaven.'"

345. There are several other stories in the Gospels that point to the possibility of Jesus eating after the resurrection, but they are not as explicit that Jesus ate food: Lk 24:30; Jn 21:9-15.

346. Fulton Sheen, *The Mystical Body of Christ* (Notre Dame: Ave Maria Press, 2015), 29.

347. For an excellent summary of how Augustine speculated what the resurrected body might look like, see David Hunter, "Books 21 & 22: The End of the Body: Heaven and Hell in the *City of God*," in *The Cambridge Companion to Augustine's City of God*, ed. David Meconi (Cambridge: Cambridge University Press, 2021), 276-96.

348. James Hannon, *Holy Viaticum: A Historical Synopsis and Commentary* (Washington, D.C.: The Catholic University of America, 1951), 1-2; Wirix, "The Viaticum," 248.

349. Grumett, *Material Eucharist*, 200-202.

350. Hannon, *Holy Viaticum: A Historical Synopsis and Commentary*, 8.

351. Wirix, "The Viaticum," 251 n. 9.

352. Wirix, "The Viaticum," 251. See also n. 9.

353. Pitre, *Jesus and the Jewish Roots of the Eucharist*, 82.

354. Pitre, *Jesus and the Jewish Roots of the Eucharist*, 77-115.

355. Pitre, *Jesus and the Jewish Roots of the Eucharist*, 98-99, 107.

356. Eusebius of Caesarea, *The History of the Church*, trans., G.A. Williamson (New York: Penguin, 1989), 6.44; Hannon, *Holy Viaticum: A Historical Synopsis and Commentary*, 8-9.

357. Wirix, "The Viaticum," 251-53.

358. Wirix, "The Viaticum," 253.

359. Kasza, *Understanding Sacramental Healing*, 198.

360. Catholic Church, *Catechism of the Catholic Church*, 1324.

361. Irwin, *Models of the Eucharist*, 102.

362. John Paul II, *Ecclesia de Eucharistia*, 5.

363. Ratzinger, "Eucharist, Communion, and Solidarity," 83.

364. The United States Conference of Catholic Bishops, "Seven Themes of Catholic Social Teaching."

365. Thomas Aquinas, *Summa Theologica*, IIa-IIae q. 58 a. 1.

About the Author

Stuart Squires is the Director of the MAPM Program at St. John's Seminary, the seminary for the Archdiocese of Los Angeles, California. He earned his Ph.D. from the Catholic University of America, his M.A. from the University of Chicago, and his B.A. from DePaul University. He has published in a variety of academic journals, including *Annales Theologici*, the *Journal of Greco-Roman Christianity and Judaism*, *Augustinianum*, the *Scottish Journal of Theology*, *Cistercian Studies Quarterly*, *The Heythrop Journal*, and *Augustiniana*. In 2019, he published *The Pelagian Controversy: An Introduction to the Enemies of Grace and the Conspiracy of Lost Souls*.

FOCOLARE MEDIA

Enkindling the Spirit of Unity

The New City Press book you are holding in your hands is one of the many resources produced by Focolare Media, which is a ministry of the Focolare Movement in North America. The Focolare is a worldwide community of people who feel called to bring about the realization of Jesus' prayer: "That all may be one" (see John 17:21).

Focolare Media wants to be your primary resource for connecting with people, ideas, and practices that build unity. Our mission is to provide content that empowers people to grow spiritually, improve relationships, engage in dialogue, and foster collaboration within the Church and throughout society.

 Visit www.focolaremedia.com to learn more about all of New City Press's books, our award-winning magazine *Living City*, videos, podcasts, events, and free resources.

NEW CITY PRESS